Creative Units
for the
Elementary School
Teacher

Edward F. DeRoche
and
Erika Gierl

Creative Units
for the
Elementary School
Teacher

Parker Publishing Company, Inc.

West Nyack, N.Y.

PRINTED IN THE UNITED STATES OF AMERICA

B & P

A Word
from the Authors
About This Book

First of all, this book is based on the belief that elementary teachers want to be creative and imaginative. For this reason, we seek to expose you to these teaching ideas so your creative imagination can be stimulated to develop additional and more productive activities.

Second, we feel the material in these chapters will help stimulate children's thinking and enhance their learning as well as providing variety and a change of pace.

Third, we believe that children in every classroom should be exposed to learning situations which go beyond the textbook. Experience with different media can improve the development of skills, the attainment of positive attitudes, and create the excitement that is too often absent in the learning process.

Fourth, the materials and problems developed in this book are encountered daily throughout our adult lives. If we expect children to utilize and appreciate the knowledge and understanding offered by these chapters, the teacher must be the one to strike that initial spark of interest.

In light of this, the value of this book to both teacher and pupil will become evident. Specifically for the teacher, the units and activities enhance the potential for successful teaching. The material, because of its uniqueness as a teaching aid, provides a ready means for motivation. Once a teacher has the class motivated, the activities and materials help to make the learning of specific skills interesting and meaningful.

There is general agreement that the unit approach to teaching and learning is most effective and efficient. This book is based on that premise. The authors have also designed many units as "teaching units" rather than "resource units" so that the teacher can prepare lesson plans directly from the book. However, you may wish to select and use those activities which are immediately useful or pertinent to the subject matter currently being taught in your classroom. This will help supplement, enrich, and expand your present instructional program. Resources such as tests, films, filmstrips, books, recordings, free materials follow each unit for your convenience.

We urge you to try these activities and units and note the reaction of your students. You will find the children eager, motivated, interested, and learning more than you realize.

A book of this nature will help the good teacher make her classroom a center of attentive students. With imaginative approaches, children easily become interested and excited about their learning.

EDWARD F. DEROCHE
ERIKA GIERL

Contents

1. **Using Daily Newspapers to Stimulate Learning** . .   1

    The daily newspaper as an invaluable aid in the teaching process. How to develop classroom activities using newspapers for developing skills in mathematics, science, language arts, and social studies.

2. **Magazines: A Ready-Made, Effective Teaching Aid** .   19

    The style, color, and content of magazines make them a valuable addition to materials used by the teacher and learner. Effective ways the teacher can use magazines to increase learning skills.

3. **Using Actual Road Maps for Instruction**   30

    The use of road maps in teaching language arts, social studies, and arithmetic.

4. **Developing Skills Through a Variety of Reference Books**   46

    Catalogues, directories, atlases, dictionaries, and encyclopedias serve as the basis for many teaching ideas.

vii

4. Developing Skills Through a Variety of Reference Books (continued)

Teachers can use these activities to supplement the language arts and arithmetic programs.

5. Imaginative Teaching with Travel Folders **71**

Take your children through the exotic lands illustrated in travel folders. Use the activities in this chapter to open the doors to the world. Discover that travel folders can also be utilized to develop skills in various subject matter areas.

6. Ideas and Sources for Units on Conservation . .   **87**

This group of units provides teachers with guidelines leading to pupil involvement in conservation and appreciation of their natural environment. There are many national programs in this area today, however their eventual success depends largely upon public support and public action. Children will become aware of this civic responsibility with actual problem-solving situations as suggested here. The units in this chapter deal with air, water, soil, wild life, scenic beauty and other resources.

7. Teaching Everyday Economics to Children . . .   **119**

One of the new frontiers in the social studies area is the inclusion of planned experiences with everyday economics. These experiences are drawn from within the youngsters' range of living. Each child is a participant in the economy no matter what the size or extent of his role. Teaching basic concepts and their application is important. Teachers will be able to use these units to advantage because the activities cut across many subject matter areas, including the law of demand, banks, savings, loans, interest, credit, taxes, etc.

8. **Exploring the New Frontiers: Outer Space and Oceanography** **156**

Man is exploring the universe from the depths of the sea to the far reaches of space. This chapter provides units that will enable teachers and children to join the adventure of probing into the unknown. The topics dealt with here are "Space Exploration," "Project Apollo," "Astronauts," and "Oceanography-Sealab II."

Index **221**

Chapter 1

Using Daily Newspapers to Stimulate Learning

Teachers have found that newspaper articles provide excellent supplements to textbooks. They have discovered that the daily newspaper helps the learner find meaning in what he is studying. Used properly, it can serve to stimulate interest in practically any subject matter area. Students usually relish assignments using this medium, and approach "old" tasks with "new" enthusiasm.

The use of the newspaper as a teaching aid should not be confined to a current events period. It should be used as an integral part of the daily program. Youngsters should be encouraged to remain constantly watchful for items in the newspaper which promote better understanding of topics currently being considered in the classroom. The following unit examines the newspaper and draws from it a great number of interest-provoking activities.

Objectives

1. To help children become aware of, and appreciate, the newspaper as a text of our modern world.
2. To help children grasp the interrelatedness of all school subjects.
3. To help children understand the events and activities of the world around them.

1

4. To develop abilities, such as reading for content, reading between the lines, reading for discrimination, interpreting, using mathematical concepts, analyzing writing styles, etc.
5. To promote qualities of patriotism and increased respect for the American way of life.

Materials and Resources

Local newspapers should be used whenever it is possible. If the local paper does not provide sufficient coverage for all the activities listed here, it is then wise to secure the newspaper from a metropolitan area which is nearby.

For purposes of comparison it is necessary that a variety of newspapers be available for the youngsters to examine. However, for most class activities it is advisable that each child have a copy of the same paper.

Of interest to teachers is the fact that a great many newspapers will supply a classroom with sufficient copies, usually free of charge, if a newspaper unit is being undertaken.

Primary Grades

The complexity of the vocabulary and sentence structure, plus the unfamiliarity of the concepts presented in most newspaper articles makes their use very limited in the early grades. This is not to say that a primary teacher cannot find many ways in which to use this instructional tool.

The primary activities could include such things as:

▶ Studying the purpose and format of daily newspapers.
▶ Studying the function of the newspaper in our American society.
▶ Collecting pictures of persons, places, and things.
▶ Using advertisements for simple problems in arithmetic.
▶ Developing captions for pictures.
▶ Using comic strips and cartoons to develop reading skills.
▶ Reading aloud by teachers to develop social awareness through human interest stories.

Using the newspaper in this fashion could give impetus to the children's own class newspaper which could incorporate some of the features of a real newspaper, such as headlines, human interest stories, factual news reporting, announcements and so on.

The following activities will be primarily directed to the intermediate grades, but primary teachers may see possibilities for their own classes by making some minor adjustments.

Intermediate Grades

As an introduction to the unit, the teacher should discuss with the class the structure and organization of a newspaper. The following topics should be included:

> Headlines—use of key words, bold print, columns.
> Front page, editorial page, sports page, society page.
> Syndicated columns.
> Ads—classified and business.
> Articles—news, features, fillers.
> Cartoons.
> Entertainment features.

The discussion should also include the types of reading which are encountered, such as educational and recreational reading. Attention should be drawn to the variety of skills which will be needed for successful understanding, such as reading for main ideas, for details, for interpretation, and for cause and effect. Youngsters must be made aware of the use of figurative and picturesque language which they will constantly encounter.

LANGUAGE ARTS

■ Select newspaper articles or advertisements and have students read for a specific purpose, such as:

1. main idea
2. specific detail
3. implications
4. cause and effect

■ Have students find articles which point up the differences between fact, opinion and fiction. Discuss the place of each type of writing and the importance of being able to distinguish between them.

■ Select an event currently taking place in the school or the community. Divide the class into two groups. Have one group write up the event as a straight news story and the other group write it up as an editorial. Compare the styles of writing.

■ Select a series of cartoons from the newspaper. Have students interpret each cartoon in terms of its meaning. Have each student write a punch line and compare his statement with the cartoonist's statement.

■ Prepare Thermo-fax transparencies of certain cartoons and have the class discuss them, using the following questions:

1. What does the cartoon mean?
2. What symbols did the cartoonist use to make the cartoon meaningful to the reader?
3. What does the cartoon imply?
4. What is meant by the "punch line"?
5. Why does one report the news using cartoons?

■ Have students make cartoons about events going on in the school and the community.

■ Select a news story concerning some international event. Have students imagine how the story would have been written from the point of view of another country.

■ Have the students build a story around a news item. Have them try to imagine the accompanying illustrations. Some youngsters may even want to actually illustrate the story. Encourage them to do so.

■ Make a list of all figurative language used on the front page, sports page, editorial page, etc. Identify the figure of speech used. Keep on adding to the list as the unit progresses.

■ Have the children select five articles and relate the theme of each in one sentence. Longer articles may require telling in one paragraph.

■ Remove a headline from an article and have the class or each individual student write an appropriate headline for it. After the assignment, compare their headlines with the original.

■ Reverse the above process. Give each pupil a newspaper headline and ask him to write a short article based on the headline. Compare his article with the original. Discuss the purposes of headlines.

■ Remove the captions of some pictures. Have the students write a two or three sentence description explaining the picture.

■ Use newspaper articles to help students develop skills in such areas as:

1. note-taking   2. paragraph outlining
         3. finding a topic sentence

■ Use the newspaper to teach new words and their meaning by:

1. identifying new words
2. finding their meaning—by context and by using the dictionary
3. spelling new words
4. using them in a sentence

■ Have the class record in a notebook all new words and their meaning which they encounter in the newspaper.

■ Have the class prepare a list of about seventy of the most useful words they encountered in their reading of the newspaper. Prepare a spelling test on these which will be given over a period of time.

■ Have students analyze new words from the newspaper articles as to:

1. category (science words, etc.)   3. root words
2. derivation   4. prefixes and suffixes
         5. syllabication

■ Use newspaper articles to identify figures of speech, clichés, parts of speech, types of sentences, etc.

■ Have each pupil use the newspaper to find words that one uses when talking about:

1. weather   4. families
2. sports   5. animals
3. accidents   6. television
               7. war

■ Have students compare different newspapers, for format, style, coverage, etc.

■ Use newspaper articles as central topics for discussion and debate.

■ Have students write letters to the editor concerning their feelings about a particular article or event reported in the newspaper.

■ Dramatize a particular newspaper article. For example, two or more students can read an article concerning a political issue and then pretend they are the leaders involved. They then debate the issue based on the information gleaned from the newspaper.

■ Provide an opportunity for students to practice letter writing by:

1. answering classified ads
2. applying for a position
3. preparing a letter of condolence
4. preparing a letter of congratulations
5. answering business advertisements

■ Invite a reporter to discuss with the class:

1. methods of interviewing   2. outlining a newspaper article
             3. writing the article

SOCIAL STUDIES

(Many of the activities listed in the section dealing with the language arts are just as applicable in the social studies area.)

■ Have the class select an article concerning some current event and analyze it in terms of:

1. geographical implications—topography, climate, natural resources, etc.
2. historical implications—effect of past, present, future, etc.
3. economic implications—budget and taxation, industry, agriculture, population, etc.
4. sociological implications—cultural contributions, educational structure, customs, habits, attitudes, etc.
5. international relations

■ Discuss the role of the newspaper on the national, state, and local levels.

■ Compare the similarities and differences between newspapers in democratic countries and communist countries.

■ Dramatize an article, such as one on the Common Market, having each child represent a head of government and presenting the views of that government. Have students read from other media to prepare for the dramatization.

■ Write to different cities in other countries asking for sample copies of their newspapers. Compare these with papers in the United States.

■ Have students compare specific articles in a variety of newspapers noting how the same event can be reported in different ways. Compare this to using *one* text or *one* reference book. How does using more than one source help us?

■ Have class use the newspaper as a supplement to the material they are studying in their textbook.

■ Use newspaper ads to do comparison shopping. Check to see which stores offer:

1. lower prices on similar goods   3. sales
2. specials   4. off-season merchandise
5. special services

■ Have children categorize the various items in the ads as luxury items or necessities. How do we decide which is which?

■ Have the children check the business and financial section of the newspaper. Attempt to determine:

1. what effect a particular item may have on the community.
2. what effect a certain event may have on the nation.
3. how a company's future, etc., has an effect on individuals in the community.
4. how technological advances will benefit the country.
5. how business and industry are able to alter the course of a community's life.
6. how maintaining a healthy climate for business and industry benefits a community.
7. the advantages of free enterprise.

■ Start a permanent file where youngsters can collect and save articles pertaining to particular areas of study. This makes an excellent reference file for future use. Youngsters should determine the categories which might include:

1. conservation
2. air pollution
3. space exploration
4. countries—India, African nations
5. medical advances
6. urban renewal
7. local community advancements

SCIENCE

(Many of the activities listed in the section dealing with the language arts are applicable in the science area.)

■ Prepare a bulletin board posting all the articles in the newspaper that pertain to science. Have children contribute to the board for one week and then note the wide range of topics covered. Have committees study major articles and report to the class.

■ Have students collect articles pertaining to science and categorize them, such as those dealing with:

1. physical science
2. biological science
3. chemical science
4. medical science
5. space science

■ Select articles dealing with space communication and exploration and have students:

1. start a class scrapbook
2. select "space words" that should be learned
3. prepare a bulletin board on this topic
4. construct dioramas depicting a phase of space study they are most interested in
5. write a class letter to NASA requesting information on the space program

■ Have students prepare a science vocabulary notebook. Use these words in such activities as:

1. science crossword puzzles
2. science spelling baseball games
   a) mark off four bases in the classroom
   b) divide class into two teams
   c) when word is spelled correctly, student advances a base
   d) team attempts to make runs (one run for each four correct spellings)
   e) when three students from the same team miss a word, their side is out and the other team begins the spelling.

■ Have each youngster select a specific area that he is interested in (weather, space exploration, atomic energy, cancer, heart surgery, etc.), and prepare a notebook on the topic. Encourage him to use other sources in addition to the newspaper. Have him report to the class periodically on his progress—what he found, where he found it, etc.

■ Invite scientists and/or science teachers from your local area to talk to the class about the work they are doing. Have children prepare questions in advance, including some concerning items currently in the news. Have speaker direct part of his remarks to these issues.

■ Use weather maps and forecasts to trace the pattern of weather over the United States.

1. Differentiate between weather and climate.
2. Discuss the meaning of "highs" and "lows."
3. Note wind directions.
4. Note differences in temperature.
5. Note differences in humidity.
6. Attempt to predict local weather.

■ Have students find articles on cigarette smoking, seat belts and fluoridation.

1. Debate each of these issues.
2. Analyze commercial advertisements.
3. Gather supporting evidence from other sources.

■ Select articles that deal with animal experimentation.

1. Debate the use of animals for experimentation.
2. Discuss why animals are used.
3. Discuss which animals are most frequently used and why these animals are selected.

■ Supplement the science you are teaching from the textbook with science articles from the newspaper.

ARITHMETIC

■ Use newspaper ads to teach basic arithmetic facts:

1. Peaches sell for 27¢ a can. How much will three cans cost?
2. What is the price of two bunches of radishes, one quart of milk, two cans of peas and one and a half pounds of ground round steak?
3. If you purchase the above items, how much change will you receive from a five dollar bill?
4. You have $4.75 to spend on groceries. What items will you purchase in order to get the most for your money while still trying to balance your menu?
5. Add up the cost of a pair of shoes, a pair of trousers, a shirt and a jacket.

6. Subtract to find the differences between the costs of various automobiles.
7. Multiply to determine the cost of seven cans of paint.
8. Divide to find the cost of one item.

■ Use an advertisement such as the one in Figure 1-1 to develop problems. Have students make up problems also, and exchange them with other members of the class.

1. What is ceiling tile? What is the price difference between a non-acoustical tile and an acoustical tile? What does the word "acoustical" mean? Why would it be more expensive?

PANELING

CEILING TILE
First Quality 12 X 12
White....... 9 1/2¢
Acoustical...13 ¢

Rubberoid
FLOOR TILE
•Vinyl Asbestos
•First Quality
•9 X 9
•in boxes of 20
•buy by boxes $1.50

SCHOOL SUPPLY CO.
N. MAIN STREET
OPEN M-F 9 'til 9

1/4 in. Mahogany,
4 X 7, $3.40
1/4 in. Mahogany,
4 X 8, $3.80

5% discount on 10
sheets or more
10% discount on 25
sheets or more

BUY NOW! PAY LATER!
Pay $10.00 down and $20.00
per month at 3% on unpaid
balance each month.

2% delivery charge

Figure 1-1

2. What is meant by "rubberoid" floor tile? What is vinyl asbestos? Where is asbestos used? For what purposes? What is the difference in price between a box of 20 and 20 individual pieces?

3. Pretend you are building a recreation room in the basement of your home. You measure the length and width of the floor, and you find that the length is 19 feet and the width is 13 feet.

    a) What is another way of writing this? (19 x 13)

    b) How can we find the area of the floor? In other words, how much space will we have to cover with the tile? (A = L × W) What is the area of the floor? (247 sq. ft.)

    c) What is the area of one floor tile? (81 sq. in.)

    d) How will we determine the number of tiles we will need to cover the floor?

    e) What will be the cost of the tiles if we buy them in singles? By the box?

4. We want to put in a new ceiling for our recreation room. The ceiling is 17 feet by 10 feet.

    a) What ceiling tile do you think would be best? Why?

    b) What is the area of the ceiling? What is the area of each tile?

    c) How many tiles will we need to cover the ceiling?

    d) How much does it cost to cover the ceiling with acoustical tile?

    e) How much does it cost to cover the ceiling with regular tile?

    f) How much do we save if we buy regular tile? What is the percentage of our savings?

    g) If our saving is ―― per cent, do you think this is adequate, or do you still prefer acoustical tile? Why?

5. We now want to partially panel our recreation room. There are four walls, and the areas to be covered measure as follows: Wall A–9′ x 6′; Wall B–19′ x 10′; Wall C–13′ x 10′; Wall D–9′ x 3′.

    a) What does the mark (′) mean?

    b) Should we buy 4 x 7 or 4 x 8 mahogany paneling?

    c) What is the area of Wall A? B? C? D?

    d) What is the area of the 4 x 7 paneling? 4 x 8?

    e) How much more area does the 4 x 8 paneling cover in comparison to the 4 x 7 paneling?

    f) To the nearest square foot, how many 4 x 7 panels would we need to cover Wall A?

    g) To cover Wall B, how many 4 x 8 panels would we need?

    h) To cover Wall C, how many 4 x 8 panels would we need?

    i) To cover Wall D, how many 4 x 7 panels would we need?

    j) What would be our total cost if we purchased the paneling as we have described in questions f–i?

    k) Would we get a 5 or 10 per cent discount?

    l) What would our cost be with the discount?

    m) What is our per cent of savings with the discount?

6. What is the total cost of remodeling our recreation room?

7. What will our delivery cost be?

8. If we buy "on time," that is, if we paid $10.00 down and agreed to pay $10.00 per month at 3 per cent, how much will we pay each month? Complete Figure 1-2.

9. What is our total cost if we buy "on time" by making monthly payments?

Month	Down	Balance	Per Month	Balance	3% of Unpaid Balance
First					
Second					
Third					
Fourth					

Figure 1-2

10. What is our total cost if we pay cash?
11. How much do we save by paying cash? What percentage of savings is this?
12. In your opinion, is it better to pay cash for items or to buy on the monthly plan? When would you buy on the monthly plan? What suggestions do you have that would help people when they plan to buy on the monthly plan?

■ Have each student prepare three arithmetic problems using newspaper ads.

1. On a 3 x 5 card have them write the problem and clip it to the ad.
2. On a separate sheet, all problems should be completed by them with the answer circled. Have each student give you the answers.
3. Put all cards with the ads clipped to them in a box. Each student is to select three cards from the box and complete the problems for homework. If they select their own, they put it back in the box and make another selection.

■ Use the sports page to teach arithmetic concepts:

1. ratio, proportion, percentage (baseball and basketball records, won and lost records, league standings, golf scores)
2. measurement (area of athletic field)
3. metric system (international track results)
4. geometry (designs of athletic fields)
5. make a chart similar to Figure 1-3.

■ Learning to read large numbers can be more meaningful if the numbers are related to an event that is currently in the news. Cut numbers out of the newspaper and mount them on a chart.

■ Look through the paper to find Roman numerals.

1. Are they frequently used?
2. When are they used?
3. Where are we most likely to find them?

EQUIPMENT	Diameter	Circum-ference	Weight	Use
Baseball Football Puck Golf ball Soccer ball Ping-Pong ball Softball Billiard ball				

Figure 1-3

■ Use the stock market report for working with fractions.

■ Take recipes from the homemaking section and determine the amount of ingredients needed to make half a batch of cookies or a smaller cake, etc. Or figure out what will have to be done if one wants 72 cookies and the recipe will make only 24. Discuss the importance of accuracy in measurement. Discuss the importance of time and temperature.

■ Interpret line, bar, and pie graphs which are found in the newspaper. Relate findings to the accompanying article.

■ Find articles which lend themselves to graphic description. Have youngsters put the information into graph form.

■ Use the numbers in the weather news to teach addition, subtraction, etc.

TIME	7	8	9	10	11	12	1	2
TEMP.	20	22	25	32	32	33	37	32

Figure 1-4

1. How many degrees did the temperature rise between the hours of 8 and 9?
2. How many degrees difference do we see between the highest and lowest temperatures recorded?

3. Between which hours do we see the greatest increase in temperature?

Example:

	HIGH	LOW
Albany	46	40
Atlanta	75	52
Boston	52	40
Buffalo	60	40
Chicago	62	43
Cleveland	68	48
Detroit	58	40
Fairbanks	34	9
Houston	78	52
Memphis	78	51

1. Figure out the difference between the high and the low for each city.
2. Figure out the difference between the high temperatures of Memphis and Fairbanks, Chicago and Fairbanks, etc.
3. Do the same for the low temperatures.
4. Which city has the greatest difference?
5. The least difference is found in which city?

■ Culminating activities.

1. Use teacher–pupil planning in the preparation for a trip to the local newspaper office.
2. Invite editors and reporters to tell about their experiences in the newspaper business.
3. Have pupils start a class newspaper or a school newspaper.

NEWSPAPERS

References for Children

1. Ault, Phillip. *News Around the Clock.* New York: Dodd, Mead and Co., 1960.
2. Faber, Doris. *Behind the Headlines: The Story of Newspapers.* New York: Pantheon Books, 1963.

3. Faber, Doris. *Printer's Devil to Publisher*. New York: Julian Messner, Inc., 1963.
4. Lent, Henry. *I Work on a Newspaper*. New York: The Macmillan Co., 1948.
5. Meshover, Leonard. *You Visit a Newspaper*. Chicago: Benefic Press, 1962.
6. Rae, Walter. *Editing Small Newspapers: Handbook for Young Journalists*. New York: M. S. Mill and Co., Inc., 1943.
7. Sootin, Laura. *Let's Take a Trip to a Newspaper*. New York: G. P. Putnam's Sons, 1965.

References for Teachers

Articles of Interest

1. Albera, T. E. "Yes; Kindergarten Can Learn from a Newspaper Unit." *Grade Teacher*. 84:30, March, 1967.
2. Crisuolo, N. "How to Teach the Art of Reading a Newspaper." *Grade Teacher*. 82:22, October, 1964.
3. Dale, Edgar. "Preparing to Read the Newspaper." *Elementary School Journal*. 57:417-18, May, 1957.
4. Fason, W. R., and Isbitz, H. F. "Reading Activities Using Newspapers." *Instructor*. 76:24-25, January, 1967.
5. Van Ness, D. "Getting to Know a Newspaper." *Grade Teacher*. 84:104, March, 1967.

Inexpensive Material

1. American Newspaper Publishers Association Foundation, 750 Third Ave., New York, New York 10017.
Teacher's Manual—Newspaper in the Classroom. $ .75.
The Teacher and the Newspaper. $1.50.
Suggested Plans for the Study of the Newspaper in the Classroom. $1.00.
How to Get More Out of Your Newspaper. $1.00.
2. The Hartford Courant, Hartford, Connecticut.
Your Newspaper in the Social Studies. Free.
Your Newspaper in the English Class. Free.
How to Read a Newspaper. Free.

3. The Milwaukee Journal, Public Service Bureau, 333 W. State Street, Milwaukee, Wisconsin 53201.
   Catalog of Books and Pamphlets. Free.
   Catalog of Films. Free.
4. New York Stock Exchange, 11 Wall Street, New York, New York 10005.
   The Newspaper and the Investor. Free.

Films

"Democracy's Diary," 16 min., b. & w., McGraw-Hill, Inc., New York.
"Local Newspaper," 16 min., b. & w., Contemporary Films, Inc., 614 Davis St., Evanston, Illinois 60201.
"Miracle at Your Front Door," 25 min., color, Minneapolis Star and Tribune, 425 Portland Ave., Minneapolis, Minnesota 55415.

Chapter 2

Magazines: A Ready-Made, Effective Teaching Aid

The wide variety of magazines, covering almost every interest area, makes them a most useful teaching aid. Their usefulness is not confined to any one area of the curriculum, but rather serves to enhance *all* areas. Of added significance is the fact that magazines not only enlighten us regarding current issues and concerns, but also serve as a stimulating leisure time activity.

(This unit is not designed for any one particular magazine. Thus, activities are general so that most magazines could be used. No specific subject matter areas are indicated.)

Objectives

1. To acquaint pupils with the wide range of magazines that are available.
2. To enable pupils to use magazines effectively.
3. To develop and strengthen skills related to various subject matter areas.
4. To encourage wide reading, both for educational and recreational purposes.
5. To encourage the reading of magazines as a leisure time activity.

Materials and Resources

A wide variety of magazines should be obtained. The students should be encouraged to bring in magazines which they may have at home. If it is possible, enlist the aid of several classrooms in building a collection. This "library" can then be shared with the other rooms.

Primary Grades

The complexity of the vocabulary and sentence structure, plus the unfamiliarity of the concepts presented in most magazine articles make their use very limited in the early grades. This is not to say, however, that a primary teacher cannot find many ways in which to use this instructional tool. The general purpose and the format of the magazine can be presented, along with its contributing function in American society. The magazines most useful here would be those that are largely comprised of pictures.

The following activities will be primarily directed to the intermediate grades, but primary teachers may see possibilities for their own classes.

Intermediate Grades

As an introduction to the unit, the teacher should discuss with the class the structure and organization of a magazine. The discussion should also include the types of reading which are encountered, such as educational and recreational reading. Attention should be drawn to the variety of skills which will be needed for successful understanding, such as reading for main ideas, for details, for implications, and for cause and effect. Youngsters should also be made aware of the use of figurative and picturesque language which they will constantly encounter.

■ Use magazine articles to help students develop the following skills:

1. Getting the main idea by
   a) locating the topic sentence

b) outlining the article
c) paragraphing
d) organizing ideas in proper sequence
e) summarizing

2. Developing vocabulary and sentence structure by
   a) using new words for weekly spelling lists
   b) using pronouns, adverbs, and adjectives
   c) finding words that describe
   d) finding clauses and phrases
   e) finding compound and complex sentences

■ Have students select an article of interest to them and complete the following activities:

1. What is the name of the author?
2. Are his qualifications or occupation indicated?
3. What does the title tell about the article?
4. What is the first paragraph about?
   a) main idea
   b) people
   c) places
   d) events
5. Outline the remaining paragraphs as follows:
   a) main idea of each paragraph
   b) attitude author has toward problem
   c) alternatives or conclusions offered, if any
6. Summarize article
7. Rewrite the article as follows:
   a) title
   b) first sentence of each paragraph
   c) summary
8. Does your rewriting capture the highlights of the article?
   a) What clues does this give you for writing your own stories or articles?
   b) Do you see any evidence from your article that the author may have outlined the article before actually writing it?

■ Have students write an article about some topic of interest to them. Have them keep in mind a specific magazine which the article would be suited for. List the following suggestions to be used when writing:

1. Decide on a tentative title.
2. Make an outline.
3. Write the first sentence of each paragraph.
4. Fill in the paragraphs.
5. Summarize the article.
6. Make final decision on the title.

■ Using a collection of various magazines, have each student select one magazine and complete the following:

1. Name of magazine.
2. Type of magazine.
3. How often is it published?
4. What does the table of contents tell about the magazine?
5. For whom (audience) is the magazine published?
   a) Can you tell by the name?
   b) Can you tell by the table of contents?
6. Why do you think the publishers named the magazine as they did?
7. What other material is in the magazine that is not listed in the table of contents?

■ Have students read various magazines to note the following:

1. How do various magazines review books?
2. How do book reviews in magazines differ from book reporting in school?
3. Discuss with the class:
   a) Who or what is a critic?
   b) What is his role or purpose?
   c) Are critics necessary?

■ Have students write a book review following the pattern of a particular magazine.
■ Have students select a science article and answer the following questions:

1. What is the title of the article?
2. Who is the author?

3. What area of scientific knowledge does the article concern itself with?
4. What does the article tell you about the particular science subject?
5. Does the author come to any conclusions? If so, what are they?
6. List all the scientific words that are used in the article.
7. Is any of the material in this article also provided in your textbook?
   a) What are the similarities between what is said in the article and what the textbook says?
   b) Are there any differences? Why do you think these differences exist?
8. What questions did you have as you read the article?

■ Have each student carefully examine a magazine for abbreviations. Example: NASA, HEW, etc. Assign a committee to develop a master list of abbreviations and a bulletin board on the topic. Discuss:

1. The purposes of abbreviations.
2. Rules for abbreviation.
3. Categories of abbreviations.

■ Discuss with the class the purpose of magazine editorials. Examine magazines for their editorial comments.
■ Have each student select an editorial from one of the magazines and complete the following:

1. What is the issue?
2. What position does the editorial take? Why?
3. Do you agree or disagree? Why?
4. Outline the *facts* that the editor uses to support his position.

■ Have individual youngsters pretend to be the editor of a magazine. Then have them select an issue or problem and write an editorial. Encourage the use of facts to support their position or to refute an opposing position.

■ Investigate editorial topics published during the last month or two by having youngsters complete the outline in Figure 2-1. They will have to refer to back issues, possibly at the library, for this activity. At least three different magazines should be selected.

NAME OF MAGAZINE		
EDITORIAL SUBJECT	GENERAL POSITION	SUGGESTED SOLUTIONS TO PROBLEM
–	–	–
–	–	–
–	–	–
–	–	–
–	–	–

Figure 2-1

■ Compare magazines and newspapers.

1. How are they similar?
2. How are they different?
3. What is the purpose of each one?
4. When do we use one and when do we use the other?
5. Do we have need for both?

■ Select an event of international significance. Have children collect all newspaper articles surrounding this event for a period of one week. Compare these with similar articles in a weekly news magazine. Discuss these sources in regard to content, detail, and scope. Consider the function of these two sources of information. Is one superior to the other or do they serve differing needs?

■ Have children put magazines into categories.

■ Have the class select ten cartoons and answer the following questions:

1. What is a cartoon?
2. What topics do these cartoons depict?

3. What message is the cartoonist trying to provide the reader?
4. Do all the cartoons have captions? Why?

NEWS	FASHION	SPORTS
-	-	-
-	-	-
-	-	-

FEATURE	BUSINESS	TRAVEL
-	-	-
-	-	-

Figure 2-2

■ Cartoon contest. Have each student select a political or social issue of local or national significance. Have a committee select the five best cartoons depicting the situation. To do this have the committee develop criteria for good cartooning.

■ Have children look through magazines to find who the famous people are at the present time. Have the children attempt to determine why these people are important and what significant contribution they are making to our society.

■ Magazine advertisements are informative and appealing. Use ads to help students develop the skills incorporated in the following activities.

■ Select an advertisement and complete the following questions:

1. What is the product advertised?
2. What format is used to catch the eye of the reader?
3. Is there *action* in the ad?
4. What characters are used?
5. What expressions are used?
6. List all words that are descriptive.
7. List all words that are "emotion packed."
8. Is the ad believable?
   a) What makes it real?
   b) What prevents it from being real?

9. Does the ad have an illustration of some type?
   a) What does it say to the reader?
   b) Suppose the ad only had the name of the product and a picture. Would you know how the picture related to the product?
10. Select three advertisements. Cut out the name of the product and the picture that goes with it. (NOTE: Not necessarily the picture of the product itself) Have your classmates try to determine what the advertiser would say about the product in relation to the picture.

■ Have youngsters select a product. Then have them cut out other pictures, words, and phrases to make a poster of their own. Show the class how they would advertise and why.

■ Develop an art project using the color and the black and white advertisements in the magazine. Interesting collages can be made from these ads.

■ Picture reading. Cut out from magazines pictures of advertisements. Remove all writing from the ad, leaving only the picture. Have students answer the following questions:

1. What is the product being advertised?
2. How does the picture tell you what is being sold?
3. What idea(s) is the picture trying to give the reader?
4. Are some ad meanings difficult to determine because you have removed the writing? Why?
5. Is there more than one object in the picture? How do these contribute to the product being sold?
6. Does the ad catch your eye? Why?
7. Now, look at the same ads with the writing on it.
8. Do you get more meaning from the ad? Does the writing help sell the product? Are key words used? How are these emphasized?

■ Have students select a picture of a product they like and then write their own advertisement for it. Make a bulletin board or display using these ads.

■ Give each student a magazine, a pair of scissors, and the following directions. (Put the italicized words on the board.)

1. Find pictures that represent each of the following shapes. Label each picture using the words on the board.
2. Words: *rectangle, triangle, prism, cylinder, pyramid, cone, sphere, half sphere, circle.*
3. Is there a difference between the shape of a triangle and a prism, triangle and pyramid, sphere and circle?

■ Use pictures of house floor plans from homemakers' magazines to provide lessons similar to the following (see Figure 2-3):

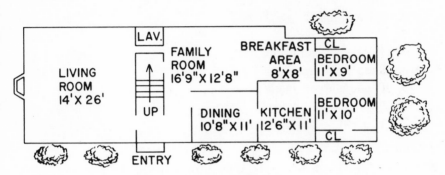

Figure 2-3

1. How many rooms does this house have? (No way to tell unless we agree there is no upstairs, yet there are stairs that say "up.")
2. What is the area of each room?
3. Is this plan drawn to *scale?*
4. What do we mean when we say a plan is drawn to *scale?*
5. On the floor plans, what does "CL" mean? What does "up" mean? What do ('), ("), (x) mean?
6. If one inch on a ruler equals six feet, how many feet can be drawn on a regular 8" x 11" piece of paper if we are drawing to scale?
7. Draw to scale (½" = 4') a floor plan for a house with the following dimensions:
   Living room: 12' x 16'
   Dining room: 8' x 16'
   Bedroom: 6' x 8'
   Bedroom: 9' x 12'
   Family room: 14' x 18'
   Kitchen: 10' x 8'

■ Have pupils bring in some "how to do it" magazines to get ideas about scale drawings for making things. Youngsters who are particularly interested in constructing smaller items should be encouraged to do so. Have finished products brought to class where pupils can explain how they put them together.

■ Scan magazines for landscaping information. Pose problems to the class related to this information, and have them attempt to solve these problems. *Examples:*

1. Bare spots in the lawn.
2. Poor drainage.
3. Poor soil conditions.
4. Tree planting.
5. Placement of shade tree.
6. Ornamental planting.
7. Erosion.

■ Use recipes from magazines to complete the following:

1. What is the name of your recipe?
2. List all the abbreviations in your recipe and tell what they mean.

   Example: 1 lb.—one pound
   ½ c.—one-half cup
   ¼ tsp.—one quarter teaspoon
   3 oz.—three ounces

3. Read the directions
   a) What does it tell you to do with the ingredients?
   b) What does it tell you about oven heat?
      (1) What does 350°F mean?
      (2) What do the symbols (°) and (F) mean?
   c) How much time is involved in preparation? In baking?
   d) Do the directions tell you how many servings your recipe will make? How many?
4. Suppose you are having more people than the recipe will serve. What will you do?
5. What will you do if the recipe makes more than you will need?

■ Use the food section to develop skill in meal planning. Use the seven basic foods as a basis. Check menus to see whether they have included the seven basic foods.

■ Culminating activities.

    1. Have children make plans to share their magazine "library" with another class.

    2. Start a class magazine.

References for Children

1. Botter, David. *News Reporters and What They Do*. New York: Franklin Watts, Inc., 1959.
2. Epstein, Samuel. *The First Book of Printing*. New York: Franklin Watts, Inc., 1955.
3. Foster, Joanna. *Pages, Pictures, and Print*. New York: Harcourt, Brace and Co., 1960.
4. Rogers, Francis. *Painter Rock to Printed Page*. New York: J. B. Lippincott Co., 1960.
5. Ryan, Leonard and Ryan, Bernard. *So You Want to Go into Journalism*. New York: Harper and Row, Publishers, Inc., 1963.
6. Simon, Irving. *The Story of Printing*. New York: Harvey House, Inc., 1965.
7. Stein, M. L. *Your Career in Journalism*. New York: Julian Messner, Inc., 1963.

References for Teachers

1. Davenport, Walter. *Ladies, Gentlemen, and Editors*. New York: Doubleday and Co., 1960.
2. Mott, Frank. *A History of American Magazines*. Cambridge: Harvard University Press, 1938.
3. Peterson, Theodore. *Magazines in the Twentieth Century*. Chicago: University of Illinois Press, 1964.
4. *Magazines in the Classroom*. National Education Association. Single copy 40¢.
5. Wolseley, Roland, E. *Careers in Magazines and Books*. Quill and Scroll Foundation, University of Iowa, Iowa City, Iowa. $10 for 50 copies, plus 75¢ postage.
6. Norman, R. B. *Magazines in the Classroom*. Magazine Publishers Association, Inc., 575 Lexington Ave., New York, New York.
7. Dale, Edgar. "The Reading of Magazines." *The News Letter*. November 1965. Ohio State University, Columbus, Ohio.

Chapter 3

Using Actual Road Maps for Instruction

Road maps can be used to teach many concepts in social studies, arithmetic, and language arts. The time to teach or use any of the activities in this chapter depends upon your program. However, you will find that many of the activities are applicable to the subject matter you are now teaching. You will also discover that the children can enjoy themselves and learn at the same time. You are encouraged to develop your own ideas and add to the material presented.

(The authors have indicated levels for each of the activities. Teachers will have to decide the readiness of their own particular group.)

Objectives

1. To enable pupils to use a road map effectively.
2. To develop an understanding of the variety of information which a road map provides.
3. To strengthen subject matter concepts through the use of road maps.

Materials and Resources

Use road maps of city, state, United States, and North America. These can be obtained in sufficient quantity so that each child may have his own. Check with service stations, oil companies, automobile associations, and the Chamber of Commerce for assistance in securing these materials.

For the primary grade activities, the material is designed only for the use of a city map. In this way we stay in the child's immediate environment.

Intermediate grade activities are based on various maps of the United States. The teacher can project many of these activities to the use of world maps or maps of specific countries.

SOCIAL STUDIES

Primary Grades

■ Have each child make a map of the classroom. Sketch in children's desks, teacher's desk, windows, doors, etc.
■ Have each child make a map of the school showing his room, the principal's office, etc.
■ Have each child make a map of his neighborhood showing the school in relation to his home, his friends' homes, etc.
■ Give each student a map of the city and have them:

1. locate the street on which they live;
2. locate the school;
3. locate the neighborhood landmarks;
4. locate major civic landmarks, such as, library, courthouse, parks, etc.
5. locate rivers, major highways, etc. that pass through the city.

■ Introduce the concept of legend by having students refer to the legends on their city maps.

1. Explain the purpose of legends.
2. Have pupils make a legend of the classroom, school and neighborhood in order to illustrate how and why legends are used.
3. Relate above experiences to the city maps they are using. Ask pupils:

   a) How does the map tell us where the parks are?

    b) How does the map tell us where airplanes land?

    c) If we want to play golf, how could we find out where to go?

    d) Suppose we are going on a trip and we want to visit an interesting place, how will the legend help us find it?

    e) How does the legend help us find the way we should travel from place to place?

■ Further strengthen the concept of direction by having pupils locate north, south, east, and west. Ask questions such as:

1. Our school is in what direction from your house?
2. In which direction will we have to go to reach the library?
3. Why do we say we live on the north side of town?

■ Teacher–pupil planning:

1. Plan a trip using the city map.
2. Outline the trip in terms of route, distance, places to visit, time, and so on. Each child may plan his own trip, small groups could plan different trips, or the entire class could plan a trip.

■ Use teacher–pupil planning and road maps to initiate a field trip.

■ Problem–solving:

1. Supposing a class of third graders from a nearby school wanted to visit us. How could we help them select the shortest and safest route?
2. How did our town or city get started? What natural features may have contributed to its growth?

Intermediate Grades

■ Run off mimeographed state outline maps, putting in major cities, major highways, capital, legend, etc. (Symbols actually tell us something.) Have pupils:

1. Find their home town or city and circle it in red pencil.
2. Find boundaries of the state.
3. Find the capital. How is it marked?
4. Find the five largest cities.

■ Compare this map with a road map of their state. Does the road map tell us more than simply location? In what ways is the road map more useful?

■ Directions: N, S, E, W, NE, etc. Where is their home city in relation to the capital? In relation to the rest of the state? To major rivers? To surrounding states?

■ Use map legends and ask:

1. Where is the legend located?
2. What is it used for?
3. What does it tell us?
4. How does it indicate differences among types of roads?
5. How does it indicate differences among sizes of cities and towns?
6. What is the scale used for?

■ List some historic places indicated on the map that a person might visit while in your state.

■ Have students circle in red pencil all points of interest they have visited in their state. Circle in regular pencil all points of interest that they have *not* visited. Now plan a circle tour to these places, originating at and returning to their home.

■ Find the airports located in the state and discuss why they are located where they are.

■ Find the railroads going through the state and discuss why they service certain areas.

■ Have the youngsters find out how road maps first began and who the people were who were instrumental in road map development.

■ Challenge the class to attempt to find at least one place in the state named for a famous person from that state.

■ Have class play "Find It." Give each student a road map of the United States. Have them place a check on the map each time they discover the answer to questions such as:

1. Find Houston, Texas.
2. Find Highway (Route) 66.
3. What large cities does Route 66 go through?
4. Find Springfield, Ohio.
5. In what direction is it from Houston, Texas?

■ Have class play "Across the Border." One student names a state and the other student indicates all the states that border it. *Ex.:* Maine, bordered by New Hampshire.

■ Have the class discover and discuss what is meant when the map tells us that a place is so many feet above sea level. Do the same with elevation. Are these two terms the same, similar, different? Are there sea level or elevation differences in the states they are studying?

■ Have the class prepare a bulletin board about each state they are studying indicating the state's name, its capital, major products, famous people, motto, nickname, governor, etc.

■ Use the road maps to locate the more significant rivers in the United States. What states do they flow through?

■ Discuss what is meant by the term "Interstate Highway." Find out:

1. How does the legend help us find them?
2. What states does Interstate 95 go through?
3. What states does Interstate 85 go through?
4. What interstate highways go through our state?
5. Where do these highways originate?
6. Where do these highways terminate?

■ Use various road maps to find the state:

1. Motto   5. Bird
2. Flag   6. Song
3. Flower   7. Governor
4. Nickname   8. Capital

■ Have students form several committees to plan an interstate trip for the class. In their plans they should include:

1. where they will take the class;
2. the means they will use to get there;
3. the route and miles each day;
4. the points of interest along the way;
5. what they expect to get out of the trip;
6. how long they will stay, and where;
7. plans for their return.

■ The committee should obtain pictures, advertisements and the like for their chosen areas.

ARITHMETIC

Primary Grades

■ After children have determined where they live and where the school and other landmarks are, develop problems such as:

1. Who lives the farthest from school?
2. How many blocks does Bill travel to get to Ed's house?
3. How many blocks will we have to walk to the library if we start at home? At school?
4. Is the distance greater or less than a walk to the nearest park?
5. How many blocks is it from Main Street to Center Street?
6. Find the shortest route from our school to Main Street.
7. How many blocks are involved?

The number and types of problems which can be developed here are endless. The problems can and should be directly related to the mathematical concepts the class is currently studying. Relating these concepts to the use of road maps makes them immediately useful and more meaningful than just the typical "Bill and Ed went to the store," etc. Teachers and children both are encouraged to make up their own problems as often as the occasion arises.

■ Have children count the number of parks included on their maps. Then have them compare the sizes of the parks: Greenfield Park is larger than Washington Park, but smaller than Grant Park. Activities such as this can be used to strengthen concepts of greater than, smaller than, more than, less than, etc.

■ The concept of intersection can be introduced by using examples such as, North Street and Center Street intersect because they have an area in common, not merely because they come together. Have children find other intersections, and tell *why* they are intersections.

■ Have children clock out a four-inch square area on their maps. Divide this area in half. What streets are found in the north half? The south half? Further divide the area into quarters. What interesting features can be found in each quarter?

■ Using a scale of twelve blocks to a mile, find out how many miles it is from one end of the city to the other, etc. If the town is too small for an activity like this, determine a scale and measure the distance from Point A to Point B.

Intermediate Grades

■ Give estimates as to how wide the state is from east to west, and how long it is from north to south. Use mileage scale to check estimates.

■ The students estimate the distance between their city or town and the capital. After each student has recorded his estimate, have him use the mileage scale and estimate the mileage in this way. Compare estimates. Is there common agreement among the students in the class? Now have students check their answers with estimations on the mileage chart of the map.

■ Using the state map and the key, figure out the population of the various counties in the state. Which counties are heavily populated? Which are sparsely populated? What factors might account for this difference?

■ Plan a 75 mile trip. What towns will you go through? Do this with a 100 mile trip. A 250 mile trip. This can be a one way trip or a round trip.

■ Work in the area of comparisons.

1. Which states have mountains? Which mountains are higher?
2. What are the different elevations in the state? Compare these. Compare elevations between states.
3. What are the approximate lengths of the major rivers. Compare these. How much longer is river A than river B?

■ Have students locate cities or states that will form the following polygons when connected:

1. triangle   3. rectangle
2. square   4. parallelogram

■ Have students use a compass and from their cities draw a one-inch circle. Two-inch circle.

1. How many major cities fall within the one-inch circle? Are these all within the same state?
2. How many states besides the one you live in fall within the two-inch circle?

■ Use straight lines to connect your city or town with other major cities. Compute mileage using mileage scale. Now determine mileage using roads and distances between points. Is there a difference? Why?
■ Have students draw a line from one arc of a compass-drawn circle through the center to the opposite arc of the circle. Explain diameter, radius, etc.
■ Use the mileage scale on the legend to measure the distance across the United States. Are the measurements in agreement with the common saying that the "U. S. is three thousand miles wide"?

1. How long is the United States?
2. How wide is it?
3. Does it matter where we choose to start our measuring?

■ Problem-solving question. If it is true that the shortest distance between two points is a straight line, then why aren't roads made in a straight line?

■ Using the mileage scale, chart out the following trip:

Milwaukee to Chicago	[ ]
Chicago to New York	[ ]
New York to Miami	[ ]
Miami to Houston	[ ]
Houston to Los Angeles	[ ]
Los Angeles to Denver	[ ]
Denver to Milwaukee	[ ]

Approximately how many miles did we travel on our trip?

■ Instead of using the story problems in the arithmetic text, develop problems relating to the use of road maps. This may be done within the framework of the current program.

Examples:

1. There are 50 states in the U. S. A. Six are called the New England states. How many states are not considered in this area?

$$50 - 6 = N$$

2. The class has 32 maps of the United States. They also have the same number of arithmetic books. How many maps and books does the class have?

$$32 + 32 = N \text{ or,}$$
$$32 \times 2 = N$$

3. Ten fifth graders went to Boston during the summer. Seventeen fifth graders went to New York.
   a) How many miles did those who went to Boston travel to get there?
   b) How many miles did those who went to New York City travel?
   c) How much farther did those who went to Boston travel than those who visited New York City?
   d) If there are thirty fifth graders, how many of them did not go to Boston or to New York City?

     e) How many miles would the fifth graders visiting New York City have to go in order to include Boston in their trip?

     f) If they flew to Boston or New York City at 400 miles per hour, how many hours would it take them to get to either place?

■ Use your map to complete chart in Figure 3-1.

STATE	CAPITAL	DISTANCE FROM YOUR CITY	DISTANCE FROM WASHINGTON, D. C.
MINNESOTA			
OREGON			
NEVADA			
TEXAS			
KANSAS			

Figure 3-1

■ Have children give examples from their map of each of the following problems. In other words, you give the problem format and they make up the problems.

    1. $40 \div 8 = N$ 3. $n + 7 = 21$

    2. $6 \times n = 24$ 4. $16 - n = 11$

              5. $15 \div 5 = N$

■ Using the mileage scale, have children give the answers to the following problems:

    1. How many inches is the scale?

    2. How many miles does it represent?

    3. How many miles does half of it represent?

    4. Why is a mileage scale valuable?

    5. How are fractions of miles indicated on the mileage scale?

    6. In what ways could map makers improve the mileage scale?

■ Working with decimals.

    1. Draw a line representing one mile.

    2. How would you indicate half of a mile?

    3. How many ways could you label it? (½ , .5)

    4. Do map makers use decimals? How?

■ While children are planning a regional or cross-country trip, explore the differences regarding time zones.

    1. Will it matter if we travel by car? By plane? By train?

    2. What adjustments are necessary for travelers? For airlines? For railroads?

    3. Why is it necessary for one country to have different time zones?

    4. How might daylight saving time add to our confusion?

LANGUAGE ARTS

Primary Grades

■ Have children develop an experience chart revolving around their use of the road maps.

■ Develop a chart with the children which lists the ways that road maps help us.

■ Have a group of youngsters give a presentation to another class regarding the use of road maps. They should organize the information and select main ideas to be presented. Good speaking habits should be stressed.

■ Have youngsters prepare skits which employ situations where one might have need of a road map, such as:

    1. coming into a strange city.

    2. looking for someone's home in an unfamiliar part of town.

    3. going on a Sunday outing.

■ Have youngsters write thank-you notes to the agency which supplied them with their road maps and point out that they should mention at least one way that these maps have helped them.

■ Have children make a booklet in which they will keep all new vocabulary words pertaining to this unit. Write a short sentence explaining what each new word means.

■ Emphasize good discussion techniques whenever children are having a group session. Make a chart showing what points a good discussion should follow.

■ Read stories to class about map making and map makers.

■ Prepare a list of states and have students find names of the states.

■ Using their maps, have the children find how many states begin with the letter C, M, L.

■ Have students list all the capitals of states in the United States in alphabetical order.

Intermediate Grades

■ Write poems about the states, but be sure to include the symbol of the state in the poem.

   Examples:

> The state of Maine
> With its big, black bear,
> Is in the northeast
> Way up there!

> In the state of Wisconsin
>   a "badger" you'll find
> No, not the animal, but
>   the men who lead-mined.

■ Have children keep an account of all new vocabulary they encounter during the course of the unit. Have them write their definitions in their own words. The list might include words such as:

1. Interstate   3. Elevation
2. Legend   4. Sea level
          5. Boundaries

■ Provide supplementary reading books about maps and map makers. Have the youngsters read and report on their findings.

■ Have the children mark the vowel sounds in the following states. Use the dictionary.

1. California	6. Washington
2. New Jersey	7. Montana
3. Louisiana	8. Vermont
4. Florida	9. Delaware
5. Arizona	10. Georgia

■ Use the dictionary to make sure of your pronunciation of state names.

■ Working with syllables. Pronounce the names of these states. How many syllables do you hear?

1. Utah	————	6. Maryland	————
2. Pennsylvania	————	7. Connecticut	————
3. Virginia	————	8. Colorado	————
4. Alabama	————	9. Arkansas	————
5. Minnesota	————	10. Nevada	————

■ How many states can you find whose names have one syllable? Two syllables? Three, and so on.

■ Have students write letters to the State Development Commission, State and Local Chamber of Commerce, and State Capitols for information on a state they would like to study. Have the letter meet all the requirements of good letter writing.

■ Choose five groups to compete in playing "anagrams." Put a state or its capital on the board and have each group try to make as many words as possible from the letters of the word on the board. *Example:* Nevada: van, ade, dean, etc. (NOTE: each letter can be used only once, or if you prefer, each letter can be used more than once.)

■ Have students write riddles using the state names from the map.

■ Solve the following puzzle using the map. Write in the correct state or capital where there is a line.

THE GREAT RACE

Sam and Charlie had a race all around the United States. Sam started at Mt. Katahdin in the East (————). Charlie started at the Alamo in the Southwest (————). It took

Sam three days to go to the Everglades (————). But Charlie took just as long to get to the home of Lincoln (————). From here Charlie went to the races at Indianapolis, ————. His next stop was to buy a car in the automobile center of the world. (————).

In the meantime, Sam was on his way to see the Statue of Liberty in ————, ————. From there he went to the capital of the United States, ————, where he met the President. He went to Gettysburg, ————, to the steel capital of the world, ————, ————, and then drove up to the resort famous for its water falls, ————, ————.

It was here that he met Charlie, who had taken a boat from Detroit to New York on one of the Great Lakes, ————. It was now that the decision would have to be made! If you had to decide, whom would you give the prize to, Sam or Charlie?

■ Have students find some major cities in the United States that have the same name as cities in other countries. Make a list as follows:

STATE	CITY	COUNTRY
Connecticut	Hartford	England
Wisconsin	Berlin	Germany

■ Scrambled words. Have children unscramble the following letters to find the capital city. When they know the city, have them use their maps to find the state that it is in.

CAPITAL		STATE
NERDEV	(DENVER)	
OOBSTN	(BOSTON)	
RSOCAN TCIY	(CARSON CITY)	
KBCIRSMA	(BISMARCK)	
ONBAT OGEUR	(BATON ROUGE)	
YMGONREMOT	(MONTGOMERY)	
IDOMANS	(MADISON)	
TLATANA	(ATLANTA)	

■ Have students use their maps to find five cities for each of the following consonant blends:

tr	pl	dr
st	cl	ch

■ Play "Where is it?" Have the class use their maps to play this game. Organize them into teams. Put three by five cards into a box with the information listed below on each card. Each student has a turn selecting one card from the box. When it is read, each student looks for the city or state on the map and raises his hand when he finds it. The first team to score ten points is the winner. *Examples:*

> Reno: The Biggest Little City in the World
> Mount Rainier National Park
> Independence Hall in Philadelphia
> Mount Rushmore National Memorial

■ Have each student select a state and write it vertically. Using his map, the object of the activity is to write horizontally a word that tells something about the state. The letters of the state should begin or end the word. *Example:*

> *M*OUNT KATAHDIN
> *A*UGUSTA
> *I*NDIAN RESERVATION
> OCEA*N*
> *E*LKS

■ Or for variety, allow letter to appear anywhere in the word. *Example:*

> *U*TAH LAKE
> SALT FLA*T*S
> S*A*LT LAKE CITY
> BRIG*H*AM YOUNG

MAPS

References for Children

1. Asimov, Isaac. *Words on the Map*. Boston: Houghton Mifflin Co., 1962.
2. Brown, Lloyd Arnold. *Map Making: The Art That Became a Science*. Boston: Little, Brown and Co., 1960.
3. Brown, Lloyd Arnold. *The Story of Maps*. Boston: Little, Brown and Co., 1960.
4. Colby, C. B. *Mapping the World: A Global Project of the Corps of Engineers, U. S. Army*. New York: Coward McCann, Inc., 1959.
5. Epstein, Sam and Beryl. *The First Book of Maps and Globes*. New York: Watts, 1959.
6. Estep, Irene. *Good Times With Maps*. Chicago: Melmont Publishers, 1962.
7. Hackler, David. *How Maps and Globes Help Us*. Chicago: Benefic Press, 1962.
8. Hathway, James. *The Story of Maps and Map Making*. New York: Golden Press, 1960.
9. Marsh, Susan. *All About Maps and Mapmaking*. New York: Random House, 1963.
10. Renkoff, Barbara. *A Map Is a Picture*. New York: Thomas Y. Crowell, 1962.
11. Tannenbaum, Beulah and Stillman, Myra. *Understanding Maps: Charting the Land, Sea, and Sky*. New York: Whittlesey House, 1957.

References for Teachers

1. Brown, Lloyd Arnold. *The Story of Maps*. Boston: Little, Brown and Co., 1949.
2. Greenwood, David. *Mapping*. Chicago: University of Chicago Press, 1964.

Chapter 4

Developing Skills Through a Variety of Reference Books

Reference books are useful tools to both children and adults, and their use requires special skills. In this unit the *emphasis* is on reference books not usually found in the classroom—catalogues, the Yellow Pages, and the telephone directory. Other reference books such as the dictionary, the encyclopedia, and the atlas are also presented.

The activities suggested are not complete. Rather, an attempt is made to show what the teacher could do with these materials. Resourceful teachers will find many more possibilities. The aspect of novelty in their use will also help serve to motivate the students.

The activities may be used all or in part, whenever wished, as they need not necessarily be taught as a unit. For instance, the catalogues could be used as supplements to the regular class work, particularly in arithmetic. It does seem important to remember, however, that most pupils will eventually use these reference books continually throughout their adult lives. They can be helped to prepare for this by spending a few minutes each week using these materials. Pupils will receive much enjoyment and learn many basic skills from a study of this kind.

Objectives

1. To acquaint youngsters with the wide variety of reference books.
2. To develop the skills youngsters will need to use these common materials effectively.
3. To develop skills in related areas by means of these materials.

Primary and Intermediate Grades

Since the skills which are being introduced or strengthened in this unit often depend on what learning has previously taken place, it is deemed wiser for the individual teacher to decide at what level any activity will be presented.

MERCHANDISE CATALOGUES

Each student should have his own catalogue if at all possible. If this is not possible, secure enough catalogues so that youngsters can work in groups of no more than three or four.

■ Have pupils find the index of the catalogue and answer the following questions:

1. What does the index tell you?
2. How does it differ from the index of a book?
3. What other information do the index pages give you?
4. What is meant by "parcel post"?
5. Does the index list parcel post rates?
6. Does the index list parcel post zones?
7. In what zone do you live?
8. What is the meaning of "C.O.D. Fees"?

■ Determining sizes.

1. To buy clothes from the company's catalogue, what does the company suggest you do?
2. Does the catalogue provide directions for measuring your body for clothes you may want to buy?

3. What do they tell you to do about determining shoe sizes?

4. From the information given, determine your size for buying a dress or a suit and a new pair of shoes. Use a tape measure or ruler where necessary.

■ Ordering merchandise.
Suppose you wanted to buy an electric toaster.

1. What would you look for in the index? What page is it on?

2. What kind of toaster would you select? (Economy priced, the finest, etc.) Why?

3. What does the catalogue tell you that will be helpful to you in purchasing a toaster?

4. What is meant by 34F6340—Wt 8 lbs. 12 oz.—$22.95?

5. Why does the company include the weight of the merchandise you are going to purchase?

■ Develop problems using the skills currently being undertaken in the arithmetic area. *Examples:*

1. Addition—Find the total cost of a water-repellent jacket ($6.95), a pair of gabardine slacks ($8.98), a cotton T-shirt ($.79), and a pair of leather moccasins ($4.25). ($20.97)

2. Subtraction—What is the difference in cost between the highest priced electric mixer ($74.95) and the lowest priced electric mixer ($21.50)? ($53.45)

3. Multiplication—Find the total cost of 4 sheets that sell for $3.49 each. ($13.96)

4. Division—Pencils sell for $2.88 a gross. What is the cost of a dozen? (24¢) Of one? (2¢)

■ Problems may be made simple or difficult to suit the individual needs of the youngsters in the class.
■ Problem-solving.
Pretend that you are going to buy a bicycle with the money you received for your birthday. You have $40.00 to spend and

you have decided to buy the bicycle through a catalogue company.

1. Find the pages on which bicycles are listed.
2. Read the descriptions of the various bicycles.
3. Which one fits your budget? How do you know that the ones you select are in your "price range"? What is your price range?
4. Select the bicycle you are going to buy. How much does it cost? What is the catalogue number? How much is the shipping weight?
5. If you want the bicycle sent directly to your home, what will the parcel post rate be?
6. In what parcel post zone do you live?
7. Read the parcel post table, find your zone number and determine shipping cost.
8. What will the total cost of your bicycle be?

■ Problem-solving.

Suppose you were going to buy a fence for the yard outlined in Figure 4-1. How would you go about buying the fencing needed?

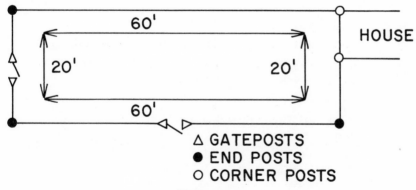

Figure 4-1

1. What are gateposts? End posts? Corner posts?
2. How many gateposts will you need for fencing the yard in the illustration? How many corner posts? End posts?

3. What is the perimeter of the yard? What is the area of the yard? Which of the two measures should you be concerned with for fencing the yard? Why?

4. How many entrances are there to the yard? How big are they?

5. The catalogue from which you are buying the fence lists prices as in Figure 4-2.

6. Do you understand the chart? If not, what is confusing to you? Clear up any difficulties before you start!

7. Select the height of the fence you wish to place around the yard. What height have you selected?

8. First, determine the number and cost of the fence posts. (Answers are for 36″ fence.)
   a) How many gateposts do you need? (4)
   b) What will be the weight of the gateposts? (48 lbs.)
   c) What will be the cost of the gateposts? ($12.40)
   d) How many end posts do you need? (3)
   e) How much will they weigh? (63 lbs.)
   f) What will they cost? ($15.75)
   g) How many corner posts do you need? (2)
   h) How much do the corner posts weigh? (30 lbs.)
   i) How much will they cost? ($7.90)
   j) What is the total weight for all posts? (141 lbs.)
   k) What is the cost for all posts? ($36.05)
   l) What is the cost of shipping the fence posts? 5 per cent per 100 lbs. 141 lbs. rounded off equals 100 lbs. Thus, 5 per cent of $36.05 = $1.80
   m) What is the total cost? ($37.85)

9. Now, determine how much fencing you will need, plus the cost of same.
   a) What is the perimeter of the yard? (Note: subtract the width of the gate entrances 160′ − 10′ = 150′)
   b) How many feet of fence will you need to go around the entire yard? (150′)
   c) What will be the approximate weight of the fence? (½ of 309 lbs. = 154 lbs.; 154 lbs. + 309 lbs. = 463 lbs.)
   d) How much does one foot of fence cost? (62¢)

FENCE HT. INCHES	GATEPOSTS CAT.NO.	WT.LBS.	PER POST	CORNER POSTS CAT.NO.	WT.LBS.	PER POST	END POSTS CAT.NO.	WT.LBS.	PER POST
36	13F29	12	$3.10	13F41	15	$3.95	13F50	21	$5.25
42	13F30	13	3.45	13F42	16	4.45	13F51	23	5.75
48	13F31	14	3.75	13F43	18	4.75	13F52	25	6.25

CHAIN LINK – STRONG LAWN FENCE

HEIGHT IN INCHES	CATALOGUE NUMBER	WEIGHT PER 100 FEET	PER FOOT
36	R13F60NF	309 lbs.	62¢
42	R13F61NF	339 lbs.	68¢
48	R13F62NF	368 lbs.	73¢

NOTE: For these problems the shipping cost is 5% per 100 lbs. Round off to nearest 100 lbs.

Figure 4-2

    e) How much does 150 feet of fence cost? ($93.00)

    f) What will be the shipping cost? (463 lbs. rounded to 500 lbs.; 5 per cent per 100 lbs.; 25 per cent per 500 lbs.; 25 per cent of $93.00 = $23.25)

    g) What will be the total cost of the fence (without posts)? ($116.25)

10. Total cost of fence and posts.

    a) What is the total of the fence posts? ($37.85)

    b) What is the total cost of the fence? ($116.25)

    c) What is the total cost for posts and fence? ($154.10)

11. Did we forget anything? (Yes, gates!)

12. Catalogue information for gates (Figure 4-3).

CHAIN LINK FENCE GATES

HT. IN.	WIDTH FT.	CAT. NO.	SHPG. WT. LBS.	GATE
36	4'	13F4N	23	$ 13. 25
42	4'	13F5N	24	13. 85
48	4'	13F6N	27	14. 35
36	6'	13F4M	40	$19. 95
42	6'	13F5M	43	21. 50
48	6'	13F6M	46	23. 75

Figure 4-3

13. How many gates do you need? (2)

14. What widths are the gates you need? (1—6′; 1—4′)

15. What is the weight of the two gates you need? (63 lbs.)

16. What is the cost of the gates you need? ($33.20)

17. What is the shipping cost for gates? (63 lbs. rounded to 100 lbs., thus 5 per cent of $33.20 = $1.66)

18. What is the total cost of the gates? ($34.86)

19. What is the total cost for the entire project of fencing the yard? ($154.10 + $34.86 = $188.96)

20. Develop a similar problem of your own. Have some of your classmates do the same. Exchange problems.

■ Have several different kinds of catalogues available. Have children compare them in terms of:

1. Content
2. Variety of merchandise
3. Price ranges
4. Prices on similar items
5. Layout, eye-appeal, general attractiveness
6. Readability
7. Shipping costs

■ Form committees to draw up lists of products available for use.

1. in the kitchen.
2. on a camping trip.
3. in various sports (golf, hunting, etc.).
4. in a home workshop.
5. in the garden.
6. in lawn care.
7. in automobile maintenance.
8. in various hobbies.

■ Vocabulary building.

1. Have students find pictures in the catalogue that would serve as an example of each of the following words:

quilts	humidifier	bassinets
dinette	antifreeze	genuine
dinnerware	generator	petite
shelving	easel	bicycle
blender	rechargeable	umbrella
lanterns	portable	flannel
aluminum	television	furniture
percale	insulated	mattresses
swivel	seamless	washable

2. Using the word and the picture, write an advertisement which will promote interest in buying the product.

■ Have youngsters write letters to the mail-order firm for various reasons, such as:

1. Asking to exchange goods for different reasons, (wrong size, etc.).
2. Defective merchandise.
3. Merchandise damaged in shipment.
4. Dissatisfaction with merchandise.
5. Misrepresentation of claims made.
6. Overcharge for merchandise.
7. Wrong order received.
8. Order not received.

■ Discuss with the class the merits of buying through a merchandise catalogue. List the advantages and disadvantages. Compare it with buying by other methods. Discussion should include such topics as buying with cash and on credit, quality of merchandise, making economic choices, etc.

YELLOW PAGES OF THE TELEPHONE DIRECTORY

■ Have each student obtain a copy of the Yellow Pages from their home or from the telephone company. Old copies are most useful.

1. What is the purpose of the Yellow Pages?
2. How are the Yellow Pages arranged?
3. Do your Yellow Pages have a civic section? If so, what does it tell you?
4. Do we find an index here? Is this index similar to a book index? An index in a merchandise catalogue?

■ The Yellow Pages tell us about places and things. These are arranged under headings or topics, in alphabetical order.

1. If you wanted to know where to buy a dishwasher, what heading would you look under? (dishwasher)

   2. If you wanted to buy a guitar, what heading would you look under? (musical instruments)

   3. If you wanted to find the address of the F.B.I., what heading would you look under? (U. S. Government)

■ Where to find it?

Each student suggests a product, such as "paste." Other members of the class find the product in the Yellow Pages. The first one to find and identify the product has a turn to name a product.

■ "Let your fingers do the walking."

To play this word game, find the word that best illustrates the description.

   1. "I rhyme with fear. I'm used in cars, trucks, and trains. You'll find me between F and H in the Yellow Pages." What am I? (gear)

   2. I cover well, and when put on I sometimes smell. I also make old things new. What am I? (paint)

   3. In the yellow pages you will see a list of places to buy me. I am something you should wear. So look carefully, I am there. (shoes, coat, dress, etc.)

■ Using the pronunciation key in Figure 4-4, select five words for each column. Use words from the Yellow Pages.

ärm	āge	câre	ĕnd	ĭll	Īce	ōld	ŏdd	cūbe
1.								
2.								
3.								
4.								
5.								

Figure 4-4

■ Compound words. Select a page from the Yellow Pages and list all the compound words you can find on the page. Write these on a separate sheet of paper. Who has the longest list? Are they all compound words? What is a compound word?

■ Form committees and divide the Yellow Pages into sections, one group taking A to D, etc. Have each committee go through their section and list all the *services* offered. Youngsters should place a check (√) behind each service they were not aware existed.

1. Each committee should share their findings with the rest of the class.
2. Each committee may select one unusual service and present it in pantomime. The rest of the class tries to guess what service it is.

■ Have children select an interesting advertisement and respond to it by making a telephone call or by writing a letter.

■ Have youngsters make posters advertising a product or service. Work for uniqueness, originality, and good use of descriptive words or phrases.

■ Check the restaurant section of the Yellow Pages. What nationality groups are represented? Plan an outing to one of these restaurants, perhaps in conjunction with a social studies unit. Send a class letter requesting a menu. Inform the proprietor in advance, when you expect to arrive and how many are in your group.

TELEPHONE DIRECTORY

■ Have each student obtain a copy of the telephone directory.

1. How does the telephone directory help us?
2. How is it arranged? (alphabetical order)
3. What other information is found in the telephone book? (emergency numbers, zip code numbers, area codes, etc.)
4. What are area code numbers? How do they help us? What is your area code number?

■ Discuss proper telephone usage. Dramatize everyday telephone conversations. Have class evaluate the situation.

■ Have each student practice one of the following:

1. Proper procedure for answering the telephone.
2. Calling long distance.
3. Making an emergency call to the fire department.
4. Calling the police department to report a stolen bicycle.

■ Have the youngsters explain in their own words the types of calls listed below:

1. Station-to-station	4. Collect calls
2. Person-to-person	5. Mobile and marine service
3. Conference calls	6. Overseas calls

■ Alphabetical order. Put the following names in alphabetical order as they would be listed in the telephone directory.

Cassidy, Edward J
Cassidy, Edward F
Cassidy, Audrey
Cassidy, Alice
Cassidy, Joseph
Cassidy, Kathy
Cassidy, Peter
Cassidy, Eileen
Cassidy, John M
Cassidy, Edward R
Cassidy, Florence Mrs.
Cassidy, Victor
Cassidy, Robert W
Cassidy, Mary C
Cassidy, John M Jr

■ Using the zip code area map. Have children draw up their own individual list of friends, relatives, etc.

1. Check the correct addresses of persons on the list.
2. Find the zip code area in which the address is located.

■ Have children make their own personal telephone directory. Include name, address, telephone number, area code, and zip code.

■ Make posters demonstrating the proper use of the telephone.
  1. Display them.
  2. Have small groups of children visit other classrooms with the posters and explain them.

■ Long distance rates.
  1. How much does it cost to call someone living in the state capital if you call at 9:00 A.M. on a Monday morning?
  2. How much more will it cost if you call person-to-person?
  3. Should you call person-to-person or dial direct? Why?
  4. How much do you save by dialing direct and talking only for three minutes?
  5. Do you save money by calling at different times of the day or night? At what times will you save the most money?

■ Figuring cost. What would your phone bill be if you made the following calls? (Rates based on Milwaukee, Wisconsin)
  1. Arizona, Phoenix—
       3 minutes—6:10 P.M.—Monday   —cost ($2.45)
  2. Minnesota, Rochester—
       3 minutes—5:00 P.M.—Tuesday   —cost ($ .85)
  3. Michigan, Detroit—
       3 minutes—9:00 P.M.—Wednesday—cost ($ .60)
                                                    (Total $3.90)

■ Overseas calls. Does your phone book tell you the approximate cost of calling someone in another country? If so, about how much would it cost to call Australia? Panama?
■ Secure a "Tele-Trainer" kit from the local telephone company. If the local company does not have such a kit, request that they contact the nearest Bell System office. This kit contains valuable teaching aids for the language arts, science, and social studies areas.
■ Teacher–pupil planning. Plan a field trip to the telephone company. Prepare a list beforehand, of the things to look for and the questions that will be asked.

DICTIONARY

■ Discuss the dictionary and its uses with the class.

1. What is a dictionary?
2. When should it be used?
3. How is the dictionary arranged?
4. What is the pronunciation key in the dictionary used for?
5. Make a list of all of the types of information the dictionary contains.

■ Alphabetical order. Have students put the following words into alphabetical order.

keystone	kidnap
kick	keynote
key	kidney
keyboard	kid

■ Use other lists for similar purpose, to give youngsters experience with alphabetical order.

■ Finding root words. Have students find the root word of each word in the following list:

auditorium	biography
describe	geography
auditors	bibliography
transcribe	intermission
telegraph	commission
transmission	

■ Game of prefixes. Have the class separate into five teams. Each child may use his own dictionary. Put a prefix on the board (ab, ante, re, trans, etc.). Each team then has two minutes to list as many words as they can using that prefix. The team with the longest list wins. A variation would be to have each student work on his own.

■ Game of suffixes. Each student in the class uses his dictionary to try to win this game. Put a suffix on the board (age, ance, ant, etc.). Each student then has ten minutes to list all the words he can ending with the suffix on the board. The student with the longest list wins the game. A variation would be to have the class divide into teams to develop the list.

■ Have students select a letter of the alphabet. Using all the words listed under this letter in the dictionary, have each student complete the chart in Figure 4-5.

B

ANIMALS	SPORTS	FAMOUS PEOPLE
baboon	badminton	Beethoven
beaver	boxing	Brahms

PLANTS	MUSICAL INSTRUMENTS
begonia	bagpipe
burweed	bugle

Figure 4-5

■ Animal hunt. Have each student in the class use his dictionary to find the name of the animal described.

1. Found in the desert, this small animal is related to the spider, and is poisonous. The first letter in the word *spider* will give you a clue. (scorpion)
2. A large goat that lives in the mountains of Europe, Asia and Africa, this animal will look you in the eye (i). (ibex)
3. Sometimes sounds like a laughing animal, he lives in Africa and Asia. (hyena)
4. A bright colored tropical bird with a very large beak, the clue is "you, *too, can* find him in the dictionary." (toucan)

■ Treasure hunt. Have the class use their dictionaries to hunt for the treasures found on the path (Figure 4-6). Each word tells the prize they will win. After each word, in the space provided, have students tell what the word means, what it is.

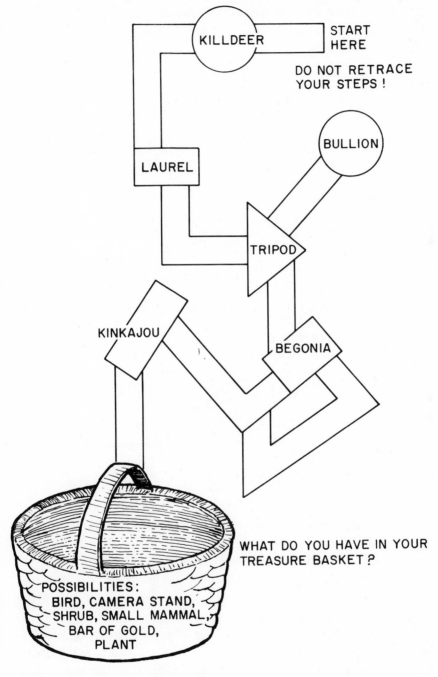

Figure 4-6

■ Have students open their dictionaries to any page they desire. When they have selected a page, ask them to complete the following activities:

1. List the words that have one syllable, two, three, four, five.
2. Pick out words that describe something or someone. Make a list of these words.
3. Find and list the words that are nouns, verbs, adjectives. Does the dictionary provide clues to the parts of speech of words?
4. Find and list words which tell that something moves or does something.
5. Find words that have long vowel sounds of a, e, i, o, u, short vowel sounds of a, e, i, o, u.
6. Find words on your page that can be made into a new word by changing the first letter. Example: boy, toy; rain, pain; went, tent.
7. Find words that have double vowels that are the same. Example: feet, food, pool.
8. Find words that have two vowels together that are not the same. Example: head, tail, cruel.
9. Find words that have double consonants.
10. Find and list words that end in by, ing, ed, ly.
11. Find and list words that are compound words.
12. Make a list of all of the new words that you encounter.

■ Guide words. Discuss the use and purpose of guide words.

1. Develop a list of words. Have youngsters find each word in the dictionary and list the guide words found on that page.
2. Develop activities similar to the one in Figure 4-7. The word in Column I comes between which pair of words in Column II?

■ Have youngsters make their own dictionaries using vocabulary currently being used in the social studies and science areas. Include definitions for each word and then have the word used in a sentence. Keep adding new words as they arise.

COLUMN I		COLUMN II
1. elaborate	(B)	A. eel - egg
2. elect	(C)	B. egg - elastic
3. effect	(A)	C. elastic - elected
4. eight	(B)	
5. effort	(A)	

Figure 4-7

ENCYCLOPEDIA

■ Have youngsters become acquainted with the encyclopedia by explaining the organization, purposes, and uses of the volumes.

1. Review alphabetical order.
2. Explain the numbers and letters on the binding.
3. Point out multiple entries and cross references. Example: Otter, Animals, Mammals.
4. Emphasize the importance of proper use of this reference tool. It is *one* source of information. Other sources should also be considered when researching a topic.

■ Have students use the encyclopedia to discover how the alphabet and number systems were developed. Prepare a bulletin board on this topic; example—"The Alphabet In History."
■ Where are they?
Have students use the encyclopedia to locate and find information concerning:

1. active volcanoes—names and countries
2. highest point on the earth—name and country
3. lowest point on the earth—name and location
4. largest island on the earth—name and location
5. seven wonders of the world
6. first library

■ The tale of two cities.
Prepare a box in which there are slips of paper with the names of major cities of the world on them. Have each student select from the box two slips, and complete the chart in Figure 4-8.

COMPARISON	(PARIS)	(LONDON)
LONGITUDE		
LATITUDE		
COUNTRY		
CONTINENT		
LANGUAGE		
POPULATION		
AREA IN SQUARE MILES		
MONEY-NAME		
U.S. EQUIV.		
TYPE OF CLOTHING		
POINTS OF INTEREST		
CLIMATE		
TEMP. AND RAINFALL		

Figure 4-8

■ A country of your own.

Have each student select a country (Jordan, Israel, etc.), and prepare a booklet on this country using the encyclopedia for pertinent information. Provide the following outline as a guide.

Form of Government	Famous People
Capital	Area
Head of State	Location
Names of Leaders	Chief Products
Official Language	National Problems
Flag	International Problems
Money	National Holidays

■ Know your government.

Have each student select a division of our national government from the following list. Then, prepare a booklet and/or an oral report that will be presented to the class.

Department of Interior
Department of Health, Education and Welfare
Federal Bureau of Investigation
Immigration and Naturalization Service

Internal Revenue Service
Civil Rights Division
House of Representatives
Senate
Supreme Court
Presidency
Cabinet

■ Have each student select one volume of the encyclopedia and search for names of people who have made contributions in the following fields of study:

1. Astronomy   4. Biological sciences
2. Medicine   5. Physical sciences
3. Space travel   6. Geological sciences
            7. Chemical sciences

■ Who invented what?

Have each student select a volume from the set of encyclopedias in your classroom or library and complete the chart in Figure 4-9.

Have a committee compile the findings.

INVENTOR	INVENTION	DATE AND PLACE OF INVENTION

SIGNIFICANT EVENTS LEADING UP TO INVENTION	USES OF INVENTION

IMPACT ON THE LIVES OF THE PEOPLE

Figure 4-9

■ The body.

Students can gain much information on various parts of the body; where they are, how they work, their functions, etc. Assign each student one of the following topics for which he is to prepare a chart and an explanation:

kidneys	trachea
joints	epiglottis
gall bladder	spinal column
stomach	muscles
esophagus	duodenum
palate	pancreas

■ Hobbies.

Have each student select a hobby or science subject of interest to him and research the subject by

1. gathering information on the subject
2. gathering pictures and other items on the subject
3. making a booklet on the subject

Use the encyclopedia, *plus* supplementary materials.

■ Have the students use the encyclopedia to tell what the words in Figure 4-10 have in common. After each column, have them tell how these words differ. List meaning next to each word.

I	II	III	IV	V	
foil	Franc	feldspar	lynx	Loire	
épée	Mark	granite	lark	Rhine	
saber	Peso	quartz	lamb	Volga	
___	___	___	___	___	COMMON
___	___	___	___	___	DIFFERENCE

Figure 4-10

■ Biography.

Discuss with the class the meaning of the word *graph*. Ask: What is an autograph? A biography? An autobiography? Have each youngster select a person of interest to him (Jack London, John F. Kennedy, etc.), and write a short biography on the person selected. Discuss the contents of a biography with the class before giving this assignment. Use the encyclopedia and other references for background material for the biographical sketch.

■ Parts of speech.

Ask: Does the encyclopedia provide any information about the parts of speech? Have each student make a list of the parts of speech and tell what the encyclopedia has to say about each one. The chart in Figure 4-11 may be helpful.

PARTS OF SPEECH	DEFINITION	USE	EXAMPLE
NOUN			
PRONOUN			
ETC.			

Figure 4-11

■ Punctuation.

The encyclopedia provides some interesting information concerning punctuation. Have each student complete the chart in Figure 4-12.

PUNCTUATION MARK	SYMBOL	WHEN USED	ENCYC. EXAMPLE	YOUR EXAMPLE
PERIOD	.			
COMMA	,			
COLON	:			
ETC.				

Figure 4-12

■ Sports.

Have each student select a sport from the list below and trace the history of the sport as described by the encyclopedia.

baseball	judo	tennis
pole-vaulting	football	track
swimming	boxing	squash
high jumping	fencing	golf
handball	curling	hockey

■ Greek and Roman mythology.

Have students use the encyclopedia to complete the chart in Figure 4-13.

GREEKS MYTHICAL PEOPLE	WHAT DID EACH NAME SYMBOLIZE TO GREEKS?	WHAT ENGLISH WORDS ARE DERIVED FROM THEM?
ZEUS		
PROMETHEUS		
VULCAN		
PANDORA		
MINERVA		
VENUS		
MERCURY		
GRACES		
ETC.		

Figure 4-13

■ Select one of the above and find more information by using additional sources.

■ Encourage the wise use of the encyclopedia. Develop charts and posters highlighting proper usage of this reference tool. Do not limit its usefulness to purely informational reading, but expand its use to motivational and recreational reading as well.

ATLAS

■ Have students attempt to discover the origin of the name "atlas." Discuss the purpose and uses of the atlas.

■ Have students select an atlas and turn to the table of contents.

1. What are the contents of the atlas?
2. What does the atlas tell us that other reference books do not?
3. When would you use an atlas?

■ Select a map from the atlas.

1. What does the legend tell us?
2. Is there a scale of miles? How long is it in inches? How many miles does it represent?
3. How does the legend mark the capital? Boundary lines?

■ Explain the purpose of letters and numbers around the maps in the atlas. (A, B, C, 18, 19)

1. What is the purpose of the numbers?
2. What is the purpose of the letters?
3. Do the maps indicate latitude and longitude?
4. What is latitude? Longitude?
5. Why do map makers use latitude and longitude?

■ Have the children choose a country. From the information given in the atlas, have them attempt to determine

1. geographical features   2. political features
3. climatological features.

■ After this is completed, have them check their data with that in a textbook or an encyclopedia.

■ Use the atlas to supplement the wall maps and the maps found in the textbook when teaching social studies, etc.

References for Children

1. Bartlett, Susan. *Libraries*. New York: Holt, Rinehart and Winston, 1964.
2. Buchheimer, Naomi. *Let's Go to the Library*. New York: G. P. Putnam's Sons, 1957.
3. Meyer, Edith Patterson. *Meet the Future: People and Ideas in the Libraries of Today and Tomorrow*. Boston: Little, Brown & Co., 1964.

References for Teachers

1. Barton, Mary. *Reference Books*. New York: Enoch Pratt Free Library, 1966.
2. Boyd, Jessie. *Books, Libraries, and You*. New York: Charles Scribner's Sons, 1941.
3. Cook, Margaret. *The New Library Key*. New York: Wilson Co., 1963.
4. Kouns, Robert. *How to Do Library Research*. Chicago: University of Illinois Press, 1966.
5. Morse, Grant. *The Concise Guide to Library Research*. New York: Washington Square Press, 1966.
6. Murphey, Robert. *How and Where to Look It Up*. New York: McGraw-Hill, 1958.

Chapter 5

Imaginative Teaching with Travel Folders

Travel folders open the doors of the world to elementary school pupils. The content found in travel folders provides a different kind of learning experience for the student. The language is descriptive, the pictures are interesting, and the ideas are fascinating.

As a teacher you will find that travel folders help to motivate students because of their novelty and attractiveness. Assignments will become more meaningful because of the uniqueness and content which travel folders provide. And yet, with all this, nothing will be lost in the subject matter content or skills areas. You are still teaching reading, social studies, and arithmetic, but you can be confident that the students will respond to your teaching with greater enthusiasm.

Objectives

1. To provide teachers with novel materials for teaching subject matter concepts.
2. To provide activities for pupils in subject matter areas utilizing travel folders.
3. To further develop basic skills necessary in other areas.
4. To help convince students that learning can be fun.

Materials and Resources

Travel folders are available in unlimited forms and varieties. They can be obtained from numerous sources, such as travel agencies, airlines, automobile associations, railroad lines, bus lines, and steamship lines.

Primary and Intermediate Grades

Since the skills which are being introduced or strengthened in this unit often depend on what learning has previously taken place, it is deemed wiser for the individual teacher to decide at what level any activity will be presented.

SOCIAL STUDIES

■ Start a collection of travel folders. When a sufficient number have been acquired, have each student develop a notebook on a country of interest to him.

■ In his notebook, have the student plan a trip for one or two weeks in the country of his choice. Decisions should be made on the basis of the information in the travel folders.

1. How will he get there?
2. What will be the estimated transportation costs?
3. What points of interest will he plan to visit while in that country?

■ Prepare an outline map of the United States or Europe, etc. (about 10′ x 7′). Have each student select a state or country and cut out material from travel folders about that area and glue this material to the map. Each student can report to the class why certain cutouts were placed on the map.

■ Have students read the travel folders for specific information that is

1. historical   3. political
2. geographical   4. sociological

(Explain to the class what these terms mean.)

■ Compare the information regarding things to see and visit as listed on a road map with those listed in a travel folder.

1. Which of the two provides more information concerning places to visit?
2. What does the road map tell that the travel folder does not?
3. What does the travel folder provide that is not included on the road map?

■ Where are the most famous vacation spots in the world? (Hawaii, Bermuda, New York City, etc.)

1. Have students suggest reasons for the popularity of these areas.
2. What makes an area a famous vacation or visiting place?
3. Can we find places that are less famous but still offer a variety of attractions?

■ Where is it?
Have students answer the following questions:

1. Where is Bermuda?
2. Is it an island? Why?
3. Where is it near?
4. Who governs it?
5. What is its main import? Export? Industry?
6. Is this information found in travel folders? If not, where did you get the answers to the questions?

(Provide similar activities for Hawaii, Disneyland, Grand Canyon, Monaco, Switzerland, etc.)
■ Have each student start a picture collection of the state or country they selected. Use these to supplement the material found in the travel folders.

1. Provide a description of the physical features of the country or state you have selected. (Hills, valleys, rivers, mountains, seashore, etc.)
2. What hemisphere is it in? On what continent? Is it bordered by oceans? By other countries?

3. Is it north, south, east, or west of where you live? What
is its latitude and longitude?

4. Does the above information provide clues as to the type
of weather or climate you will find there?

■ Have children make pictures, using crayons or watercolors, of
the landscape they expect to see in the place they have selected.

■ Have children make a bar graph of the average daily rainfall
and temperature of the area they have selected. Do these factors
have anything to do with the attraction of the area?

■ Famous people.

For the state or country you have selected, does the travel
folder provide information about famous people who came
from there?

1. If not, why not?

2. Try to discover through library research some famous
people who came from the state or country you selected.

■ Culture—art and music.

Does the travel folder provide clues as to the type of art or
music that comes from the country you have selected? Where
else might you find this information? What kind of art and
music does the country you selected provide for the world?
Can you find examples (pictures, etc.) to tell the class about?
To put in your notebook?

■ Many students have never been on an airplane nor do they
know what the interior looks like. Have a class representative
write to various airlines for information and pictures.

■ Discuss with the class how travel by people of different countries would help us understand each other in a better way.

■ Discuss the following problem: If people from other countries
visited our city, what would we show them and have them do so
that they would better understand Americans?

■ Have class discuss how they should act as tourists.

1. In their own country.   2. In other countries.

■ Discuss the various means of traveling to and from places. Include:

1. types of transportation
2. factors that determine which means of transportation will be used

   (*a*) cost   (*c*) time
   (*b*) distance   (*d*) preference
   (*e*) availibility—is there an airport, railroad station, etc.?

■ Collect as many travel folders as possible centered around one particular place. *Example:* Spain.

1. Set up a display of travel folders.
2. Put up posters children have made.
3. Display items that children bring in; ceramic bulls, lace mantillas, flamenco guitar records, castanets, etc.
4. Display map showing round trip route from their hometown to various ports of call, on to Spain and back home again.

■ Arrange field trips to one or more of the following:

1. an airport   3. a bus terminal
2. a railroad station   4. a harbor

■ Make use of travel folders to supplement the textbook wherever possible when teaching social studies.

LANGUAGE ARTS

■ Have children write letters to various agencies requesting travel folders.
■ Read your travel folder carefully!

Underline all the new words you encounter. How many words did you underline? Do you know what each word means? If not, use your dictionary to help you. Now reread the sentence in which the new word appears! Does it have greater meaning for you?

■ Using the travel folders, have students find words that:

1. are compound words   4. are contractions
2. are hyphenated words   5. have prefixes
3. are abbreviated words   6. have suffixes

■ Have class analyze and discuss the meaning of the following phrases:

1. The Trip of your Dreams........
2. The Vacation of a Lifetime........
3. Live a Little........
4. Paradise Awaits You........
5. Breathtaking Beauty........
6. A Shutterbug's Delight........

■ Have students look for figures of speech in the travel folders and explain their meaning.

■ Using the dictionary, have children find out what the following words mean in relation to the travel folder information:

1. reservation   6. cruise
2. cancellation   7. passport
3. box luncheons   8. embarkation
4. budget plan   9. tourist
5. luxury liner   10. brochure

■ Have class discuss what is meant by the following terms:

1. American Plan   4. Continental Plan
2. Modified American Plan   5. Table d'Hote meals
3. European Plan   6. Smorgasbord luncheons

■ Have youngsters find words in the travel folders that make them feel happy, sad, excited! Did they find any that made them feel *sad?* Why? Why not?

■ Have children make posters, conveying feelings of happiness, gayness, excitement, etc. Use emotion arousing words or phrases to emphasize the feeling.

■ The following paragraph is representative of the material found in travel folders. The questions following it are examples of what you can do to help develop language skills in the pupils.

After a fast flight across the Blue Pacific, you will be joyously greeted in the traditional manner with fragrant flower leis. Then transportation awaits you to take you to your hotel. Here you will be met with exotic surroundings, designed with your leisure comfort in mind.

1. Underline in pencil all adjectives.
2. Underline in pen all adverbs.
3. What is a lei? How is it pronounced?
4. Should "Blue" be capitalized?
5. What is meant by "traditional manner"?
6. What is meant by "you will be *met* with"?

■ Strange words of travel.

Travel folders provide many new and strange words that students in your class will enjoy discussing. Some of these words are:

itinerary	carte blanche
accommodations	terminals
cruises	continental
gratuities	elegance
alterations	comprehensive

1. Have students prepare a folder by using an 8½" x 11" sheet of plain white paper and folding it into thirds.
2. On the front cover have them draw or glue a picture that is representative of the place the folder will tell about. Have them select appropriate wording to catch the eye of the reader.
3. On the inside pages have students use some or all of the words listed above to explain the trip.
4. On the back of the folder have students select methods of transportation and estimated costs.

■ Where am I?

Have each student use his travel folder and notebook to prepare a one paragraph description of his country, state, or place to visit. Have him read this paragraph to the class and let other members of the class try to identify the location. The student who correctly identifies the place then reads his paragraph.

■ Creative writing.

Use travel folders to provide examples of creative writing for your students. Here are two examples:

> Sublime form and color . . . a strange land of exciting beauty and adventure. And if you seek the unusual masterpieces of the Great Architect that will stir your emotions, hold you spellbound with a deep feeling of humility, then set forth for that western region of unparalleled scenic splendor.

> The landscape is positively indecent; devoid of the usual clothings of soil, grasses and trees worn by the more discreet parts of the earth's crust.

1. Discuss these descriptions with the class.
2. Have students describe the rain, waves, sun, and street in a similar manner.
3. Help them to contrast their words and ideas. Example: desert land vs. positively indecent.
4. Have them describe by means of comparison. Example: as lonely as, as sad as, as happy as, etc.

■ Synonyms, homonyms, antonyms.

The following paragraph is paraphrased from a travel folder:

         1   a   2

Another exciting day lies ahead of us. In mid-morning <u>we</u>

b   c   d

arrive at the National Park for <u>our</u> road trip. A lunch stop is

         3   4

<u>made</u> at the concrete dam. An added surprise is the boat trip

 5   e   f

around the newly-formed lake. <u>Some</u> of you will remember this

   6   7

pleasant experience.

1. Write synonyms for all words with a number over them.
2. Write homonyms for all underlined words.
3. Write antonyms for all words with a letter over them.

4. Use your travel folders. Select a paragraph and provide synonyms and antonyms for some of the words in the paragraph. Do synonyms change the meanings of these sentences? Why?

■ Sentence painting.

The wording used in travel folders provides a painted word picture for the minds of the readers. Compare these two sentences as an example:

This state provides you with a wonderful vacation that you won't believe.

A land of scenic contrasts beyond belief invites you to come and enjoy a truly different vacation experience.

1. Which sentence paints a better word picture for you? Why?
2. Now use your travel folders and paint better pictures by rewriting the following sentences.
   (*a*) Jane took a camera on her trip.

   _____

   (*b*) Take a cruise on the Great Lakes.

   _____

   (*c*) At this hotel, the accommodations are the best.

   _____

   (*d*) You will see the Grand Canyon as an erosion of nature.

   _____

   (*e*) Our school is brick colored and large.

   _____

■ Sentence structure.

Select a series of sentences from your travel folders and write down the basic parts of the sentence and the spare parts of the sentence. Then, diagram the sentence. Example:

Our people are congenial, cultured and refined.

Basic parts:	people	are	congenial, cultured, refined
Spare parts:	our		and

■ Finding and reusing the verb.

Use a series of sentences from your travel folders to select and reuse the verbs. *Example:*

This *can be* the vacation of your life.
This *can be* a way to learn about verbs.

■ Letter writing.

Using the information they have accumulated during the course of the study on travel folders, have children write letters home from the places they are visiting.

■ Dramatizing.

Have children prepare short skits involving situations encountered while traveling.

1. Making reservations at ticket counter.
2. Attempting to locate missing baggage.
3. Checking into a hotel.
4. Buying at a marketplace in a foreign country without knowledge of the language.
5. Boarding a scheduled bus in Mexico and suddenly realizing that a member of your party is missing.
6. Ordering from a menu which lists unfamiliar foods.

Encourage children to make up their own situations.

■ Form committees and have each group present a short travelogue for a television program. Have committees present a variety of approaches. For example, from the point of view of:

1. an airline.
2. a news team.
3. the local citizens.
4. world travelers.
5. the Chamber of Commerce.

ARITHMETIC

■ Reading and writing numbers.

■ Have students randomly select fifteen numbers from their travel folders and list them in Column I. In Column II, have students *write* the numbers as shown in Figure 5-1.

COLUMN I	COLUMN II
$ 639.00	six hundred and thirty-nine dollars
1,500.00	one thousand five hundred
24,352.00	twenty-four thousand, etc.
$ 12.50	twelve dollars and fifty cents.

Figure 5-1

■ Solving problems.

1. Each student in the fifth grade needs $252.90 for a round trip airplane ticket to Atlanta. There was a $5.26 tax on each ticket. How much did each child need for paying the total price of the ticket?

   ($252.90 + $5.26 = N) (N = $258.16)

2. Bert had $258.65 for a round trip ticket to Pittsburgh. Including the tax, the cost was $236.42. How much money would Bert have left after he paid for his ticket?

   ($258.65 − $236.42 = N) (N = $22.23)

3. If one railroad ticket from Milwaukee to Chicago costs $5.85, how much will it cost if six people decide to take this trip?

   ($5.85 × 6 = N) (N = $35.10)

4. If our hotel bill was $167.30 for one week, how much did we pay for one day?
   ($167.30 ÷ 7 = N) (N = $23.90)

■ Let's take a trip to Bermuda!

Have the class plan a trip to Bermuda. Everyone is going for one week. We will fly from New York's Kennedy Airport directly to Bermuda. Base all costs on adult fares. Start a travel scrapbook.

1. Shall we go first class ($145.00 round trip) or economy class ($120.00 round trip)? What are the differences? (cost, meals, seat location, etc.)

2. How much free baggage are we allowed? (Travel folder will indicate amount. Usually 44 lbs. economy class—66 lbs. first class.)

3. Do we need a passport? (No) What do we need? (Proof of citizenship for reentry to the U. S.)

4. Do we have to have reservations? (Yes)

5. Do we need a deposit? (Yes) What is a deposit? How much will we have to pay? ($25.00 each for 30 students, including teacher; thus $25.00 × 30 = $750.00)

6. Have a class member write a letter to one of the airlines making reservations. Place the letter in the class travel scrapbook.

7. Hotel accommodations. (See Figure 5-2 for rates for one week)

Hotel	Double (each)	Tax	Single	Tax
A	$115	$3.90	$125	$4.30
B	$ 72	$2.90	$ 76	$3.06
C	$187	$6.80	$201	$7.36

Figure 5-2

a) Have each student determine the cost for single rooms for the entire class for each hotel.

b) Have each student in the class determine the cost for two in a room for each hotel.

c) What hotel and what type of room accommodation would be most economical?

8. Each of the 29 students in the class has $25.64 for spending money. How much spending money does the class have in all? ($743.56)

9. Including all costs, what will be the total cost of the trip? (The answer here will vary according to the type of accommodations selected.)

10. Record this, and other information, in the travel scrapbook.

■ Flying to Honolulu.

TYPICAL FARES* FROM	JET ECONOMY	JET COACH	JET FIRST CLASS
SAN FRANCISCO	$200	$220	$285
CHICAGO	$380	$430.90	$518.10
BOSTON	$481.70	$524.50	$619.50

* 5% tax on all ticket purchases.
Round trip fares.

Figure 5-3

1. What is the difference in cost when flying to Honolulu from Boston in comparison to flying from San Francisco? (Figure the differences for each area.) Why is it more expensive to fly from Boston?

2. What is the per cent of increase when the tax is added?

3. What is the total cost of each of the above when you add the 5 per cent tax?

4. What would be the most economical flight if you flew from Chicago? Most expensive? How much more is first class than economy class? What is the per cent of increase when going first-class?

■ Seven day vacation rates.

1. Select the hotel you and your family wish to stay at. Decide whether or not you wish to use the standard or the superior rates.

2. How many in your family? If each used a single, what would the cost be? What would the cost be for a double?
3. How much is the tax?
4. What is the total cost for the seven days?
5. If you stay two extra days, what will the cost be for each member of the family?
6. What will the cost be without the tax?
7. What will be the total cost for nine days including the tax?

VACATION HOTELS		STANDARD*	
		PER PERSON	EXTRA DAYS
THE TROPIC	SINGLE	$57.00	$5.00
	DOUBLE	$75.00	$8.00
THE ISLE	SINGLE	$57.00	$5.00
	DOUBLE	$69.00	$7.00
THE REEF	SINGLE	$60.00	$5.50
	DOUBLE	$81.00	$9.00
		SUPERIOR*	
		PER PERSON	EXTRA DAYS
THE TROPIC	SINGLE	$65.50	$5.75
	DOUBLE	$85.00	$9.00
THE ISLE	SINGLE	$73.00	$7.00
	DOUBLE	$91.00	$10.00
THE REEF	SINGLE	$73.00	$7.00
	DOUBLE	$103.00	$12.00

* Tax of 4% payable to hotel on checkout.

Figure 5-4

■ Many airlines now operate passenger service on what they call the "Family Plan." For example, on one airline Dad pays full fare, Mom pays two-thirds fare, and each child under the age of 22 pays one-third fare. Using the chart in Figure 5-5, answer the following questions.

ROUND TRIP TO SAN FRANCISCO	COST DAD	COST MOM	TOTAL FOR CHILDREN	TOTAL COST
ATLANTA $252.90				
BOSTON $217.65				
CINCINNATI $257.85				
DALLAS $170.90				
DENVER $117.95				

Figure 5-5

1. Fill in the chart for each city. Assume a family of six— dad, mom, and four children.
2. How much less does it cost for a family of six living in Denver and flying to San Francisco, than another family living in Atlanta and flying to San Francisco?
3. What would the cost be for a family of six living in each city on the chart if no family plan was available?
4. How much money does the family plan save each family in each city as compared to no family plan.

■ Select data from the travel folders that lends itself to graphic illustration. Make bar graphs, pie graphs, etc. to present information more clearly and vividly, and to give youngsters meaningful experiences with interpretations of this type. Add these graphs to the travel scrapbook.

TRAVEL

References for Children

There are several travel series that are excellent references for the elementary school child. They are listed below with the countries they include.

1. *The Land and People Series.* New York: J. B. Lippincott Co. Afghanistan, Argentina, Australia, Austria, Balkans, Belgium, Brazil, Canada, Ceylon, China, Denmark, Egypt, England, Fin-

land, France, Germany, Greece, Holland, Iceland, India, Indonesia, Ireland, Israel, Italy, Japan, Mexico, Norway, Philippines, Poland, Portugal, Scotland, South Africa, Spain, Sweden, Switzerland, and Venezuela.

2. *My Village Series.* New York: Pantheon Books.
   Austria, Greece, India, Ireland, Israel, Italy, Norway, Spain, Switzerland, and Yugoslavia.

3. *The Young Traveler Series.* New York: E. P. Dutton and Co., Inc.
   Holland, Sweden, France, Switzerland, England, Wales, New Zealand, Austria, China, Scotland, South Africa, Norway, United States, India, Pakistan, South Seas, Germany, and Italy.

4. A series of books by Miroslav Sasek featuring many of the outstanding cities of the world. Macmillan.

5. A series of books by John C. Caldwell which uses the "Let's Visit _____" approach. Day.

References for Teachers

1. Gunther, John. *Inside Africa.* New York: Harper Brothers, 1955.
2. Gunther, John. *Inside Asia.* New York: Harper Brothers, 1942.
3. Gunther, John. *Inside Europe.* New York: Harper Brothers, 1962.
4. Gunther, John. *Inside Russia.* New York: Harper Brothers, 1958.
5. Gunther, John. *Inside South America.* New York: Harper Brothers, 1967.
6. Gunther, John. *Inside the U.S.A.* New York: Harper Brothers, 1947.
7. *Life World Library.* Time, Inc.

Chapter 6

Ideas and Sources for Units on Conservation

It has been said that breathing the air in our major cities for one day is a lung cancer hazard comparable to smoking two and a half packs of cigarettes. About 88 million motor vehicles are pumping more than 300 thousand tons of poisonous gases into the air per day, so that one of the necessary conditions for life, *air,* is being contaminated.

Our industrialized society has also contributed to the pollution of our water supply. For example, in 1962 about five million fish were killed because of polluted waters. One newspaper has referred to its waterways as the "Land of Stinking Waters."

The problems of soil erosion have been multiplied by man's desire to build houses, shopping centers, and metropolises. Poor soil conservation practices are seriously affecting man's food supply and that of other animals and plants.

Our last chance for conserving our natural resources rests with the education of *all* citizens. This then becomes the responsibility of teachers. To help you, we have included units on conservation with a somewhat different approach. Rather than providing the usual material, we are emphasizing pollution of the air, water, and soil. We are asking you and your class to examine the conditions of our environment as they are today and then to investigate and study each of these areas. The result, we hope, will be a greater understanding of the needs for conservation education and practices.

Objectives

1. To help develop an appreciation of the resources found in our environment.
2. To help students understand the need for wise use of air, water, and soil.
3. To show that there is a serious danger of polluting our environment.
4. To examine the contribution of individuals, public agencies, and private organizations in the area of conservation.

In this section of the chapter we are providing activities that will help you introduce the general topic of conservation. The following activities will provide background information and stimulate interest in the three succeeding units. Treat them as initiatory activities and use them to launch studies of the specific sub-topics.

Initiating Activities

■ Discuss with students the differences between conservation and preservation. Have students provide examples of each. Ask them to list those agencies and/or organizations that are concerned with conservation and those that are concerned with preservation.

■ How did the idea of conservation take hold in America? Have students investigate the beginning of the conservation idea.

■ Why do we have national parks? Have a group of students prepare a report on national parks—their origin and development.

■ Invite a conservationist to talk to the class. Each state usually has resource people from the Conservation Department who might be available.

■ Discuss with the class those things that they can do immediately which will contribute to the objectives of conservation.

Examples:

- *a*) conserve grass by using the sidewalks
- *b*) check leaky faucets and pipes
- *c*) don't be a litterbug, pick up for others
- *d*) start a conservation club
- *e*) read, write and discuss conservation with others

■ Ask boy scouts and girl scouts to tell what scouting teaches them about conservation.

■ Plan outdoor study trips for the class. Provide as much outdoor activity as possible. This is where one learns about conservation.

■ Have a student locate the Conservation Pledge. Have students take the pledge to conserve our national resources.

■ Have student representatives write to the following agencies for information:

U.S. Department of Agriculture, Forest Service, Washington, 25, D.C.

U.S. Department of the Interior, Soil Conservation Service, Washington 25, D.C.

U.S. Department of Agriculture, Soil Conservation Service, Washington 25, D.C.

U.S. Department of the Interior, Bureau of Reclamation, Washington 25, D.C.

U.S. Department of Health, Education, and Welfare, Public Health Service, Washington 25, D.C.

Country Beautiful Foundation, Waukesha, Wisconsin

National Wildlife Federation, 1412 Sixteenth St., N.W., Washington 6, D.C. Booklet on Bounties, and "Conservation Clubs for Juniors" and "Conservation News"

Conservation Education Association, Eastern Montana College of Education, Billings, Montana

The Conservation Foundation, 30 East 40th St., New York, N.Y. 10016

National Audubon Society, 1130 Fifth Ave., New York, N.Y. 10028

U.S. Department of the Interior, Fish and Wildlife Service, Washington 25, D.C.

Sierra Club, 1050 Mills Tower, San Francisco 4, Calif.

■ Have each student select one man on this list and prepare a report on the man's contributions to conservation and include some facts about his life.

a)	John J. Audubon	g)	George P. Marsh
b)	Daniel C. Beard	h)	Sterling Morton
c)	Hugh H. Bennett	i)	John Muir
d)	Bernard E. Fernow	j)	Gifford Pinchot
e)	George B. Grinnell	k)	John W. Powell
f)	William T. Hornsday	l)	Ernest T. Seton
	m) Charles R. Van Hise		

■ Have students draw posters depicting the importance of conservation.

■ Have students prepare exhibits of the conservation materials they have collected.

■ Prepare debates or panel discussions on issues in conservation, e.g., industry's contribution to pollution.

■ Vocabulary development.

Have each student develop a vocabulary list of words on conservation. Encourage each student to buy a small notebook or some 3 x 5 index cards to record his words. Whenever possible, include these words in spelling tests or written assignments.

SUGGESTED WORD LIST

pollution	watershed	erosion
conservation	oxygen	irrigation
preservation	transpiration	industry
interdependence	chlorination	detergents
adaptation	fluoridation	reservoirs
silt	respiration	aeration
filtration	distillation	desalinization

■ The following animals are in danger of becoming extinct— whooping crane, California condor, bald eagle, buffalo, mountain lion. Have students find out why these animals are rare when they were once so plentiful.

AIR POLLUTION

Shelley once said: "Hell is a city much like London—a populous smoky city." This could now be said of most of our major cities. Air is no longer that free, pure stuff of a generation ago. Presently, it is being polluted at an ever increasing rate.

This unit explores only two questions. Why is the air being polluted? What can we do about it? Hopefully, students will come to realize that work has to be done to keep our air supply adequate for plants and animals. This work entails knowing the facts, investigating hypotheses, and telling others about their knowledge.

Objectives

1. To develop an awareness of the seriousness of air pollution.
2. To develop an attitude of concern for the future welfare of our nation.
3. To encourage interest and participation in affairs of local and national concern.

Developing the Unit—Informational Activities

Problem: How and why is America polluting the air?

Generalization: Most air pollution is the result of a highly industrialized society.

Content:

► Polluted air results from
1. industrial wastes
2. vehicle exhaust fumes
3. furnace fires

► Smog
1. dirty air that blankets cities
2. a blend of smoke and fog

► Air pollution causes the following:
1. damage to plants and animals
2. corrosion of metals and other materials
3. property depreciation

Informational Activities

- Have students prepare a class *fact sheet* on air pollution. The fact sheet may contain such information as:
  1. Automobiles throw pollutants into the air equal in weight to a line of cars stretched from New York to Chicago.
  2. In some cities, breathing the air for a day is equal to smoking over two packs of cigarettes.
  3. Smog has killed people in London, England; Donora, Pennsylvania; Meuse Valley, Belgium; Los Angeles, California; etc.

- Have some students prepare a chart showing what the Clean Air Act (1963) is attempting to do.
- Have students write to friends or relatives in major cities. Ask them to describe the smog that may exist there.
- Have each student prepare pollutant boxes. Each student obtains a small box and places white tissue in it. Leaving the box open, have students place the boxes in various areas throughout the school and at home. Check each box every day to see how much dirt has been deposited in the box. Ask students to discuss their findings in relation to our lungs, breathing, filtering, etc.
- Have a faculty member who smokes blow the smoke he has inhaled into a white handkerchief. Ask the students to discuss the results. Why can it be said that smoking is like carrying your own pollution with you?

Problem: What can you do about air pollution?

Generalization: Each person has the responsibility to be both concerned and active in matters of conservation.

Content:

► Your responsibility is to

1. be informed
2. be interested
3. write letters
4. ask questions
5. teach others

Informational Activities

• Prepare and distribute a "Conservation Newsletter" written and developed by members of the class. Assign each student a task such as reporter, editor, printer, artist, or distributor.
• Have committees of students write to the following agencies for information on their activities to combat air pollution.

1. Los Angeles Air Pollution Control District
2. U.S. Public Health Service
3. Illinois State Air Pollution Control Board
4. New York City's Air Pollution Control Dept.
5. National Association of Manufacturers

• Have students survey their friends, relatives and others on their knowledge of air pollution. Prepare a "survey sheet" for their use.
• Invite political representatives, scientists, and conservationists to talk to the class about their views on air pollution.
• Have students discuss the problem of allowing the car motor to operate within a closed area (garage). Carbon monoxide is poisonous and causes death.
• Have students secure newspaper and magazine articles on air pollution. Have them find pictures of smog in Los Angeles, New York City, etc. Have them find pictures of industrial smoke.

- Poster contest: Have members of the class conduct a school poster contest on air pollution. Have the class invite three people to be the judges. Have students prepare the rules for the contest and its publicity in advance of the contest. Ask local banks or stores to display the winning posters.
- Writing contest: Have students prepare stories or essays on the topic of air pollution. Request the local newspaper to publish as many as they are able.
- Writing letters: Review the guidelines for good letter writing. Then, have students write letters to state and federal officials (Senators, Representatives, etc.) requesting information on their views and planned actions concerning air pollution.
- Debate: Have students prepare a debate on the following topic:

    Resolved: That an air tax be charged of each adult. Have members for or against the proposition seek material to support their position. Example: There is a tax on water. Should there not be a tax on air? Tax money collected for the use of air could be returned to each state's air pollution control department.

WATER POLLUTION

With over 70 per cent of our planet's surface covered by water, it seems strange that we should be talking about conserving water. It is important, however, that we distinguish between water and water that is useful. What has caused this crisis over useful water? Specifically, the industrial revolution caused the change from pure to polluted waters. Factories sprang up around our water ways, and towns and cities grew around these industrial plants. Water was used by the manufacturers to produce their products. The waste materials from these products were exuded back into the river or stream. The towns and cities used the waterways to carry away their wastes and sewage. "After all, the river is always flowing," they said, "therefore it carries away the waste products. How can you pollute running water?" Yet, history is witness to those polluted conditions less than two hundred years later.

It is now our responsibility to see to it that the waterways are clean and that water is not wasted. The water drought in the eastern part of the United States between 1961–1965 indicates our concern.

This unit explores four problems of water pollution. After establishing the importance of water in our daily lives, the unit investigates the water cycle and various conditions that cause water pollution. The unit concludes by focusing on how you and your class can begin making contributions to the area of conservation.

Objectives

1. To understand man's dependence on water and other natural resources.
2. To appreciate the need for water conservation.
3. To understand that water pollution is everybody's problem.

Developing the Unit—Informational Activities

Problem: Why is water so valuable?

Generalization: Water is necessary to all living things.

Content:

► Value of water

1. Health
   a) helps body make use of food
   b) carries food materials to cells
   c) carries waste products away
   d) blood is mostly water; two-thirds of our body weight is water
2. Industry and power
3. Irrigation
4. Transportation
5. Fishing industry
6. Recreation

Informational Activities

- Living things are mostly composed of water. Have each student bring in a sample of a fruit or vegetable.

  1. Cut thin slices from each of the samples the students bring in.
  2. Using a balance scale (grams) have students record the weight of the slices of fruit or vegetable.
  3. Place these slices in the open air for a day or two.
  4. Have students record the weight again. What happened?
  5. Have students calculate the fraction of water in the slice of fruit or vegetable.

- Have students make posters showing how rain water eventually gets to the kitchen faucet.
- Have students prepare a chart showing how water is used for recreation. Have them find a picture for each activity.
- Have students survey a local grocery store or supermarket and list all foods which are related to the fishing industry.

Problem: In what ways is the earth supplied with water?

Generalization: The earth has several sources of water supply.

Content:

► Water cycle

  1. ocean air takes on water vapor
  2. winds carry moist air to land areas
  3. moist air condenses, clouds form
  4. further cooling results in precipitation as rain, sleet, hail or snow
  5. rivers eventually flow down to the sea
  6. (plants return moisture to air by transpiration)

► Other water sources

  1. Surface water
     a) running water; streams, rivers, etc.
     b) standing water; lakes, ponds, swamps, etc.

2. Ground water
   a) below earth's surface
   b) in rocks and underground pools
   c) limited supply; must be replenished
   d) water table
      (1) upper limits of ground water level
      (2) rises in rainy season
      (3) lowers in dry season
   e) watershed
      (1) an area where water flows into the same body
          of water; surface water flows into a particular
          lake, stream, etc.
      (2) the Mississippi River has a watershed of about
          800 million acres; other examples—a gentle
          slope, the Continental Divide, etc.
3. Plant transpiration
   a) all green plants give off water vapor—plant leaves
      serve this function
   b) large tree in warm weather may give off hundreds of
      gallons of water in vapor form

Informational Activities

• Have students investigate the legend and lore of rainmakers. Is
  there a similarity between the rainmakers of old and present
  day methods of cloud seeding?
• Have students make posters illustrating the water cycle.
• Water Table. Have students illustrate water tables in a way
  similar to Figure 6-1.
• Have each student prepare a map of their community. Indicate on the map areas of surface water, watershed, water
  pumping stations, etc.
• Show the films:

  Adventures of Junior Raindrop—U.S. Dept. of Agriculture,
      8 minutes.
  Lifeblood of the Land—U.S. Forest Service, 24 minutes.
  Man's Problem—Encyclopaedia Britannica Films, 19 min-
      utes.
  Nature's Plan—Encyclopaedia Britannica Films, 14 min-
      utes.

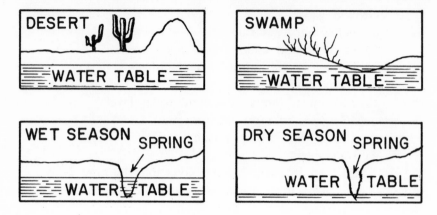

Figure 6-1

- Transpiration experiment.

    If you have a terrarium in your classroom, cover it for a day or two with a sheet of glass or plain cellophane paper. If you do not have a terrarium, wrap potted plants in cellophane paper. Have students observe what has happened to the glass cover or cellophane paper. (Water droplets will form.) *Ask:* How did this occur? (Plant leaves give off water vapor. Vapor condenses on cool surfaces.) *Ask:* Of what importance is this to other plants and animals?

- Do water plants give off oxygen? Place some water plants in separate glasses of water. Place in the sunlight. *Ask:* What happens? (Bubbles of oxygen appear.) *Ask:* How is this related to plants and animals which live in the water? *Ask:* How do fish, for example, use the oxygen supplied by water plants for breathing. (Gills absorb oxygen from the water.)

- Have students observe fish in an aquarium. Why do they keep opening and closing their mouths? Is the opening and closing of the mouth related to other movements of the fish?

- Ecology of plants and animals. Students can appreciate the relationships of plants and animals by studying the relationship between water plants and animals. Have students find out why water plants need animals and why animals need plants.

- Have students relate these findings to land plants and animals. What are the similarities? Differences?
- Have students make posters and charts illustrating these relationships.
- Discuss what happens to this relationship when water becomes polluted.

Problem: What are the causes of water pollution?

Generalization: Water pollution is primarily caused by man and is often the result of his activities.

Content:

▶ Major causes of water pollution

1. Silt—soil from the land is carried into the streams and rivers—affects water life

2. Sewage—It has been said that U. S. sewage disposal plants are adequate to serve about 70–80 per cent of the people using them—example, a sewage plant in Wisconsin deposited two million gallons of raw sewage while treatment plant was being repaired.

3. Industry—
   a) industries are located near water for three reasons— use water to make products, dispose wastes in water, water transportation is cheaper than railroad or truck.
   b) paper industries are worst polluters—some paper pulp industries are building purification plants.
   c) Public Health Department reports that about 12.7 million fish are killed yearly by industrial pollution.
   d) it is estimated that by 1980 industry will use about 394 billion gallons of water per day.

4. Insecticides and pesticides—a major cause of the poisoning of fish.

5. Detergents—
   a) cause pollution of streams and rivers
   b) poisonous to fish

      c) have caused water supplies to produce froth or foam on the water

      d) ban on "hard" detergents.

6. Heat—

      a) industries deposit heated water into the streams near them

      b) heated water lowers the ability of water to hold oxygen and this affects the fish—eventually the ecology of the stream is altered.

7. Other causes—

      a) radiation—radioactivity

      b) water from mines

Informational Activities

- Soil is carried by rivers and streams (silt). Have students place some sand, gravel, and clay into two or three glass jars. Fill each jar with water so that it covers the soil. Cap the jars and shake them well. Have the students explain what happens in these jars one day later. (Settlement takes place in the jar as it does in the water—clay at the top, sand in the middle, and gravel at the bottom.)

- Experiment with soil erosion as part of a cause of pollution. Remove one end of a wooden box and replace it with wire screening. Use aluminum foil to make a funnel shaped path and fasten it to the screened end of the box. Fill the box with soil and place it on a slant. Place a receptacle under the open end of the box. Sprinkle water over the soil. The water will run through the screening into the container. Find out how much soil it carried with it.

- Have students obtain samples of water—faucet, river water, boiled water, sewage water, etc. Using an eye dropper, place a drop of each sample on different glass slides. Cover with a cover glass. Place under microscope. Have students record their observations with sketches.

- Have students collect a water sample from a local pond or river. Send for a kit from the State Board of Health. They will test the sample and send back results. Study these results and outline a plan for correcting the condition, if correction is necessary.

- Camera activities.
  1. Have students use an 8 mm. camera to take films of polluted areas in their neighborhood.
  2. On the basis of these 8 mm. films, have students prepare an assembly program for the student body.
  3. Have students with snapshot cameras take pictures of polluted areas in the neighborhood or city. Prepare a school display of these pictures. Have students write captions for each of the pictures used. Have a committee of students visit the local newspaper editor to determine his interest in using the pictures.

- Have the students work on different projects or booklets. Form committees to consider the following topics:
  1. Pollution caused by industrial wastes
  2. Pollution caused by untreated sewage
  3. Pollution caused by soil erosion
  4. Pollution caused by trash and garbage
  5. Pollution-free waters

- Have youngsters compose a water conservation pledge of their own.

Problem: How can we conserve our water resources?

Generalization: Man must constantly search for ways to conserve his precious supply of water.

Content:

► Ways of conserving our water resources
  1. Finding new water sources—sea water—desalinization
  2. Prevent water runoff and flooding
     a) contour plowing
     b) ground cover
     c) dams and reservoirs

3. Protect water resources—example, Federal Water Pollutions Acts: 1948—control of pollution decided by states; 1956—action against pollution of interstate streams; 1961—federal government deals with water polluters at state governor's request

4. Methods of purification (making water usable)
   a) aeration
   b) filtration
   c) chlorination
   d) distillation

5. Ways in which individuals can help to conserve water

Informational Activities

- Have class representatives write to the following for information about their work:

  Robert Taft Sanitary Engineering Center, Cincinnati, Ohio
  Clean Water, Washington 25, D.C.

- Show the films:

  Clean Waters—General Electric Company, 21 minutes
  Your Friend the Water—Encyclopaedia Britannica Films, 6 minutes
  Soil and Water Conservation—Department of Agriculture, 10 minutes

- Ground cover helps conserve water and soil. Have students bring in four cigar boxes. (More if you plan to have entire class try this experiment.) Remove one end of each cigar box and replace it with wire screening. Place different types of soil in each box. Have students fill box A with ordinary soil, box B with garden soil or humus, box C with soil arranged in vertical rows, box D with soil arranged in horizontal rows. Have same kinds of soil for boxes C and D. Place a pan under each box. Fill a watering can with exactly two quarts of water. Use a measuring cup. Tilt boxes. Pour water into each box.

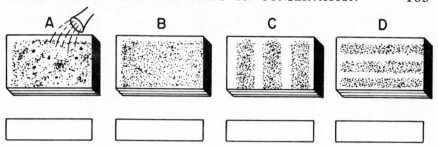

Figure 6-2

Allow water to seep into soil and run off into pans. In about one hour, pour the contents of each pan into four different glass measuring cups of one pint size. Ask: Which measuring cup has the most water? Why? What cup has the least water? Why? How does this experiment help us in our discussion of water conservation?

- Have students make posters illustrating the operation of the local water supply plant, the operation of the local sewage disposal plant, etc.
- List the names of all lakes and rivers in your local area. Complete the chart in Figure 6-3.

NAME	SWIMMING	BOATING	DRINKING	POLLUTED
LAKE-RIVER	YES-NO	YES-NO	YES-NO	YES-NO

Figure 6-3

- Invite a representative from the State Health Department to talk to the class about pollution and what the department is trying to do about it. What services are provided to communities? Individuals?
- Do all communities have sewage plants? Have students make a study of the communities in their area to find out whether

or not they have sewage plants. If not, have students find out what is done with the sewage.

- Study a river in or near your community. Starting with the *source* of the river, trace its course. What other communities does the river flow through? What are these communities doing about preventing pollution of the river in question? Have the youngsters suggest and carry out ways of finding answers to these questions.
- Visit a water purification plant.
- Brainstorming. How many ways can the class think of for individuals to help in the fight for conserving our water supply? Start off the session by filling a leaky can full of water. Compare the dripping to a leaky faucet.

SOIL CONSERVATION

American history records the many ravages of our soil. Cattlemen have been blamed for the destruction of the "sea of grass" that once flowed from Texas to Montana. The plow of the homesteader contributed to the destruction resulting in the Dust Bowl. Gold miners tore up the soil with high pressure water hoses looking for gold on the sides of hills and mountains. This devastation is illustrated by the fact that a depth of about nine inches of topsoil was covering American lands when the settlers arrived. Six inches of topsoil is average today. This amounts to a loss of about one inch of topsoil every one hundred years.

These facts led to the realization that soil conservation practices must be initiated through education and legal means. This unit provides insight regarding the nature of the problem and what is being done about it. The problems of erosion and conservation are presented in a manner which we hope will encourage further study of the situation.

Objectives

1. To appreciate the ageless process that produces soil.
2. To appreciate how important soil is to plants, animals, minerals, and mankind.

3. To appreciate that erosion control is a complicated process which can be reduced to a relatively simple formula.

Developing the Unit—Informational Activities

Problem: How is soil destroyed or wasted?

Generalization: Soil is destroyed by both man and nature.

Content:

► Soil erosion

1. wind   2. water (floods, etc.)

► Poor farming methods

1. failure to rotate crops
2. failure to use fertilizer
3. unwise plowing
4. unwise use of side hills

Informational Activities

• Have students take snapshots of land areas that were destroyed or wasted by nature (wind, water, etc.) or by man.
• Are there evidences of erosion in the neighborhood? If so, have students discuss what can be done to prevent further erosion.
• Have students find magazine or newspaper pictures illustrating good farming methods.
• After a heavy rainfall have students observe what has happened to the soil, roads, slopes or hills, etc.
• Walk around the neighborhood or local parks and record any evidences of erosion.
• Visit a farm. Find out if the farmer rotates his crop, why he uses fertilizer, what kinds of plows he uses, where his animals graze, etc.
• Show the films:

Erosion—Gateway, 10 minutes
Erosion—U.S. Department of Agriculture, 7 minutes

Problem: What are some effective soil conservation methods?

Generalization: Man has devised many ways to conserve the soil.

Content:

► Conservation methods

1. crop rotation
2. contour farming
3. terracing
4. strip-cropping
5. use of fertilizer
6. irrigation
7. planting to hold soil

Informational Activities

- Invite local farmers or their representatives to talk to the class about farming.
- Planting! Have students plant dry bean seeds under the following conditions:

  Pot A: topsoil—watered each day
  Pot B: subsoil—watered each day
  Pot C: topsoil—watered each day and sprinkled with commercial fertilizer

Have students record the differences in growth each month.

- Fill two flat wooden boxes with soil. Plant grass seed in one and leave the other box without a cover crop. Tilt the two boxes and water daily. Use a sprinkling can. Observe the effects of vegetation upon rapidity and extent of erosion.
- Plant lima beans in topsoil, subsoil and sand. Water them regularly, and record the differences in growth. Is there an initial difference? Why not? Is there a difference later on? Why?
- Have students investigate what misuses of land caused such catastrophes as the Dust Bowl in the 1930's, etc.
- Have students prepare posters illustrating soil conservation methods. Use the subject matter outline as a basis for the posters.

- Have each student plan an experiment for one of the soil conservation methods discussed in class. Have them illustrate to the class the experiment they prepared.
- Have students investigate how earlier cultures (Incas, Egyptians, etc.) farmed their land. Did they use terrace farming, strip or contour planting? List the methods that were used.
- Have class representatives write for the following:

  You Have What It Takes to Contour and Terrace and *Contour Terraces*

    Allis-Chalmers Mfg. Company,
    Tractor Division,
    Milwaukee, Wisconsin

- Show the films:

    Conserving Our Soil Today—Coronet, 11 minutes
    For Years to Come—Castle, 22 minutes
    Top Soil—U.S. Department of Agriculture, 10 minutes

Problem: How do people help conserve our soil?

Generalization: There are a number of ways that people can help to conserve our nation's soil.

Content:

► U.S. Soil Conservation Service (S.C.S.)

1. Soil Conservation District—local land users develop their own soil conservation program
2. S.C.S. Agent
3. Services provided
    a) study soil types
    b) study slopes and degrees of erosion
    c) study land use and other physical features
    d) help develop land programs, etc.

► You and your classmates

1. take an interest
2. Keep America Green Program
3. obey laws

4. keep informed
5. write letters
6. understand the ecology of living things

► Others

1. teachers of conservation   4. agronomists
2. biologists   5. ornithologists
3. botanists   6. wildlife management
                        7. forests

Informational Activities

• Write to the U.S. Soil Conservation Service for literature about their services.
• Invite an agronomist to tell the class about the work he does, the experiments he conducts, the equipment he uses, etc.
• Have students make a list of the various occupations that are related to the study of plants and animals. Describe the activities of the people in those fields.
• Have students prepare an occupational "Career Day" for other students in the school.
• Have students investigate state and local laws relating to soil or land use.
• Have students prepare posters showing the relationship between soil, plants, and animals.
• Show the films:

> *Golden Secret*—U.S. Department of Agriculture, 6 minutes
> *Your Friend the Soil*—Encyclopaedia Britannica Films, 7 minutes

Culminating the Unit—Summarizing Activities

■ Invite one of the following people to speak to the class or school assembly about conservation: an industrialist, a state senator or representative, a conservationist, a forest ranger, etc.
■ Prepare a school display of all the material collected during this unit. Also have students prepare "mini-units" of the major concepts in conservation. Each group of students can then present their "mini-units" to other classes in the school.

■ Prepare a school bulletin board on conservation. Keep the bulletin board up to date throughout the year with newspapers and magazine articles and pictures about pollution, conservation, etc.

■ Have the students prepare a 15 minute radio program on conservation. Tape record the program. Present it to a local radio station and ask them for permission to have your children put on the program as a class project.

■ Prepare a class newspaper on the topic of conservation. Use student articles, cartoons, and the like to illustrate the need for a more informed citizenry concerning conservation.

Evaluation Techniques

Youngsters should be evaluated throughout the unit.

Observe youngsters to determine how well they make use of the information gathered in the unit.

Written Test on Information Gained in the Unit

1. Define in your own words each of the following:
   (*a*) conservation   (*b*) preservation   (*c*) pollution
2. As you know, soil erosion is one of the major problems in conservation. What methods would you suggest to farmers, landscapers, and others for conserving our soil?
3. Why is air pollution a major problem of every large city? List a few possible solutions.
4. Pretend you are a government lawyer presenting your case for more laws to protect our water systems. What evidence could you present to the senators to encourage them to establish water pollution legislation?
5. The following list identifies the kinds of things that pollute our waterways. Tell, in your own words, how each of the terms describes a kind of pollution.
   (*a*) silt   (*c*) sewage
   (*b*) detergents   (*d*) insecticides
                    (*e*) radioactivity
6. Tell why you like or dislike the idea of placing a tax on the use of air, similar to our water and land taxes.

7. Match the items in Column I with the definitions in Column II:

COLUMN I	COLUMN II
(a) (4) transpiration	1. a method of conservation
(b) (2) chlorination	2. a method of purifying water
(c) (6) humus	3. a study of plant life
(d) (5) ecology	4. plants giving off water vapor
(e) (7) smog	5. the study of the relationship of living things and their environment
	6. soil made up of decayed plants and animals
	7. dirty air—like clouds
	8. cause of fish poisoning

Figure 6-4

8. Explain what is meant by the statement: "Water pollution is a crisis caused by industrialization."
9. List some occupations that are related to conservation and tell what people in these occupations do. For example, an agronomist is a scientist who_____.
10. List the ways of getting people to realize the need and importance of conservation.

WILDLIFE PRESERVATION

As we read our magazines and newspapers, we frequently come across articles which relate that a species of animals is becoming extinct or is in danger of extinction. Many organizations have been formed to prevent this. As man builds roads, dams, towns, and industrial complexes, he destroys the natural habitat of the creatures who live in the wild. He upsets the *balance of nature*.

Since children seem naturally attracted to animals, a unit such as this should hold high interest for them. They should become concerned about animals and ways in which we must protect and conserve them.

Objectives

1. To become aware of wildlife as one of our most important resources.
2. To understand that all people should be involved in wildlife conservation.
3. To understand that wildlife is essential to the balance of nature.
4. To appreciate the beauty of wild animals in their native habitat.

Initiating the Unit—Motivational Activities

■ Discuss with the children some experiences that they have had with animals; pets, zoo animals, wild animals, etc. Explore what they did for these animals. What did the animals do for them?

■ Read to the class or have the class read such books as *Rabbit Hill* by Robert Lawson. Discuss ways in which people help animals. Ask youngsters what projects they might engage in, such as building a bird feeder or planting a low dense hedge to provide cover for the birds.

■ Show the films:

Heritage We Guard—U.S. Department of Agriculture, 31 minutes

Green Island of Nature—Young America Nature Center, 19 minutes

■ Have the class write to the following agencies:

Wildlife Federation
Department 11
Washington, D.C.

National Department for Wildlife Education
Department 22
Washington 26, D.C.

■ Organize a bird watchers club. Using a field guide, record the kinds of birds that members have sighted. Have interested youngsters give periodic reports with the hope of increasing class participation.

Developing the Unit—Informational Activities

Problem: Why does wildlife play such an important part in our national resource picture?

Generalization: Wildlife is necessary to many phases of our lives.

Content:

► Economic importance

1. furs—hides	4. game
2. food	5. other products
3. clothing	6. helpful to man
	7. recreation—enjoyment

► Balance of nature—animals are an important link in man's relationship to nature.
► Necessary for man's survival.
► Provide man with beauty, enjoyment and pleasure—aesthetic value.

Informational Activities

• Have the class develop charts using various classifications, such as,

1. Fur bearing animals
2. Game animals
3. Animals which provide us with food
4. Animals which provide us with clothing
5. Animals which help man
6. Birds which help man

• Have youngsters research and report to the class such instances of the "balance of nature" as typified by the *fox* and the *rabbit,* for example.

- Cite examples of how wildlife provides us with enjoyment. Bring in aesthetic qualities.
- Show the films:

  Operations Wildlife—Virginia State Board of Education, 36 minutes

  Red 14 (Wildlife Research and Game Management)—Wisconsin Conservation Department, 28 minutes

Problem: Why is the need for wildlife conservation so urgent?

Generalization: Man has not always shown wisdom in his relationships with wild creatures.

Content:

▶ Many species are becoming extinct, not only in the United States, but in the rest of the world as well.

▶ Currently in the United States, at least 78 species are reported near extinction.

▶ In 1966, Congress passed an act to attempt to preserve endangered species,

  1. when habitat is threatened with destruction, drastic changes, or severe reduction or,
  2. when subjected to overexploitation, disease, or predation.

Informational Activities

- Have youngsters write a letter to the Secretary of the Interior asking for a list of American animals which face extinction.
- Research this problem as it relates to other areas of the world. What is Africa doing about preserving her animals?
- Write to:

  The Graphic Curriculum
  41 West 42nd Street
  New York City, N.Y. 10007

Request information regarding the Animal Secrets program.

- Have committees investigate who the leaders in the area of wildlife preservation are.
- Show the films:

  Vanishing Birds—Pictura, 11 minutes
  Vanishing Herds—U.S. Forest Service, 15 minutes

Problem: What can be done to preserve wildlife?

Generalization: There are ways in which *all* citizens can aid to preserve wildlife.

Content:

▶ The U.S. Fish and Wildlife Service provides guidelines and assistance in this area.

  1. game and wildlife refuges
  2. wildlife management
  3. rebuilding fish and wildlife population
  4. add to list

▶ State and local agencies exist to handle problems.
▶ The preservation of fish and wildlife is directly related to the problems of pollution and conservation.
▶ There are many ways in which an individual citizen can help to preserve wildlife,

  1. support legislation
  2. write to senators, congressmen, etc.
  3. join or form citizens' groups
  4. start a community project
  5. study wildlife and become knowledgeable in this area
  6. begin individual projects to help birds, etc., in your neighborhood
  7. add to the list

Informational Activities

- Have class representatives write to the U.S. Fish and Wildlife Service for pamphlets and other materials which describe its activities.

- Have class representatives write to state and local agencies for literature about their function.
- Using a state map, have children block out the areas of game or wildlife refuges.
- Construct a table model of a game refuge. What kinds of natural or man-made features will it include?
- Visit a game farm where game birds are raised.
- Visit a fish hatchery.
- Using an outline map of the state or local community, indicate the kinds of wildlife found. (Similar to a product map.)
- Have the class hunt for animal tracks to uncover evidence of what animals may be around the area. Tracks can usually be found in undisturbed snow or in damp ground near sources of food and water.
- Invite a conservationist or game warden to class to discuss the importance of his work. Have him give examples of how the children can help in this work.
- Show the films:

    Field Trip to a Fish Hatchery—Coronet, 10 minutes
    Sea Otter—National Film Board of Canada, 11 minutes
    Wildlife in the Rockies—Barr, 14 minutes
    Realm of the Wild—U.S. Forest Service, 27 minutes

Culminating the Unit—Summarizing Activities

■ Make a mural depicting wildlife prevalent in the state. Background should stress the natural habitat of the animals.

■ Have committees of students develop "conservation laws" to be introduced to "Congress." Have them present the "case" to the class, with the class accepting, rejecting or amending the bill.

■ Have panels of students present information that they have gathered during the course of the unit. Organize the panels according to research problems and areas of interest to the students.

■ Have individuals or small groups prepare dioramas depicting some aspect of wildlife preservation. Display the dioramas in some central location of the school where all youngsters may view them.

■ Decide upon a project that the class can engage in which will help the wildlife of the community. This should be carefully planned and carried out. Arrangements should be made to insure that the project will be continued if the unit is concluded before the project is finished. (Remember that projects such as *feeding* must be continued on a regular basis once they are started, as wild creatures, especially birds, become dependent upon this source of food.)

Evaluation Techniques

Youngsters should be evaluated throughout the unit.
Observe youngsters to determine how well they make use of the information gathered in the unit.

Written Test on Information Gained in the Unit

1. Name five species of wildlife that are in danger of becoming extinct. For each example, give the reason why this is happening.
2. Explain what is meant by the balance of nature.
3. Present three examples of how pollution endangers wildlife.
4. Why is it important for everyone to become involved in conservation and preservation?
5. Define the following terms:

   (*a*) wildlife management   (*d*) extinction
   (*b*) game refuge   (*e*) preservation
   (*c*) game warden   (*f*) fish hatchery

CONSERVATION

References for Children

1. Archer, Sellers. *Rains, Rivers and Reservoirs.* New York: Coward-McCann, Inc., 1963.
2. Allen, Shirley. *Conserving National Resources.* New York: McGraw-Hill Book Co., 1955.

3. Bauer, Helen. *Water, Riches or Ruin.* New York: Doubleday and Co., Inc., 1959.

4. Colby, C. B. *Soil Savers.* New York: Coward-McCann, Inc., 1957.

5. Ellis, Anabel. *Man and the Good Earth.* New York: G. P. Putnam's Sons, 1958.

6. Gabrielson, Ira. *Wildlife Refuges.* New York: The Macmillan Co., 1943.

7. Gabrielson, Ira. *Wildlife Conservation.* New York: The Macmillan Co., 1941.

8. Graham, E. *Wildlife for America.* New York: Oxford University Press, 1949.

9. Green, Ivah. *Water: Our Most Valuable Natural Resource.* New York: Coward-McCann, Inc., 1958.

10. Harrison, C. W. *Conservationists and What They Do.* New York: Franklin Watts, Inc., 1963.

11. Hitch, Allen. *Conservation and You.* Princeton: Van Nostrand Co. Inc., 1964.

12. Hogner, Dorothy. *Conservation In America.* Philadelphia: J. P. Lippincott Co., 1958.

13. *Nature's Bank: The Soil.* National Wildlife Federation Inc., 1953.

14. *Plants and Animals Live Together.* National Wildlife Federation Inc., 1953.

15. Russell, Solveig. *About Saving Wildlife for Tomorrow.* New York: The Macmillan Co., 1941.

16. Smith, F. C. *The First Book of Conservation.* New York: Franklin Watts, Inc., 1954.

17. Smith, F. C. *The First Book of Water.* New York: Franklin Watts, Inc., 1959.

18. Van Dersal, William. *Water For America—The Story of Water Conservation.* New York: Oxford University Press, 1956.

References for Teachers

1. Allen, Walter. *Conserving Natural Resources: Principles and Practices in a Democracy.* New York: McGraw-Hill Book Co., 1959.

2. California State Department of Education. *Teaching Conservation in California High Schools.* Sacramento, California.

3. Carr, Donald E. *Death of the Sweet Waters*. New York: W. W. Norton and Company, Inc., 1966.

4. Carr, Donald E. *The Breath of Life*. New York: W. W. Norton and Company, Inc., 1965.

5. Colorado Game and Fish Department. *Tools for Teaching Conservation*. 1530 Sherman St., Denver 3, Colorado.

6. Dasmann, Raymond. *Environmental Conservation*. New York: John Wiley and Sons, 1959.

7. "Guide to Teaching Conservation and Resource-Use in Michigan," Bulletin No. 425, The Department of Public Instruction, in cooperation with the Michigan Department of Conservation.

8. Gustafson, A. F., Guise, C. H., Hamilton, W. J. and Reis, H. *Conservation in the United States*. Ithaca, New York: Comstock Co., 1949.

9. Highsmith, Richard, Jensen, J. G., and Rudd, Robert. *Conservation in the United States*. New York: Rand McNally, 1962.

10. Parson, Ruben. *Conserving American Resources*. Englewood Cliffs, New Jersey: Prentice-Hall, Inc., 1956.

11. Stead, William. "Natural Resource Use in Our Economy" (Study and Teaching Aids by George Fersh). New York: Conservation and Resource Use Education Project, Joint Council on Economic Education. 1960.

12. *Saturday Review*. May 22, 1965. 380 Madison Ave., New York, New York 10017. Entire issue.

13. Superintendent of Documents, Government Printing Office, Washington, D.C.
    Wildlife on the Public Lands. 35¢
    Survival Or Surrender of Endangered Wildlife. 15¢
    Focus on Clean Water. 15¢
    A Primer on Water. 35¢
    The Story of Hoover Dam. 30¢
    The Third Wave. $2.00
    The Quest for Quality. $1.00

14. U.S. Department of Agriculture. *An Outline for Teaching Conservation in Elementary School*. U.S. Government Printing Office, Washington, D.C., 1966.

Chapter 7

Teaching Everyday Economics to Children

Young children observe the economic aspects of life at a very early age, perhaps initially at the local grocery or candy store. Their introduction to such terms as taxes, banking, credit, loans and interest probably results from family problems and discussions. These terms remian vague, however, until someone clarifies the differences, explains the processes, and evaluates the implications. This is usually the responsibility of the elementary teacher.

There are several major understandings which should be fostered when teaching the units in this section. First is the relationship of economics to our form of government. Such concepts as the gross national product, supply and demand, and free enterprise, call for understanding of industrialization, conservation, affluence, labor and management. Second, the teacher has to assist children to appreciate the differences between a capitalistic, free enterprise economic system and other economic systems in today's world. Third, the teacher should help children understand that the change and growth in themselves and the world results from the interrelationships of their own talents, their ethnic, religious, and racial backgrounds, their socio-economic levels, and the relationship of these factors upon the economy of our nation.

The units in this chapter provide some of the concepts and understandings which will help students to realize that economics plays a vital role in everyone's daily life, and that a thorough knowledge of economics provides a basis for many important decisions.

SUPPLY AND DEMAND

One of the earliest systems devised to satisfy supply and demand was the barter system. Goods were exchanged for other goods and the value of these goods was determined by scarcity and demand. This system has taken on a new form through the use of a common medium of exchange called money. We use money as the means of purchasing goods and services. Price is the amount of money for which goods or services are exchanged or offered for sale. Prices are determined largely by how much demand exists and by how great the ability to supply this demand is.

Children encounter this economic principle early in life and soon make use of the barter system. Trading baseball cards, swapping marbles, running errands in exchange for treats, all are elementary forms of the above. Teachers can use these experiences as a basis for introducing more sophisticated examples of this basic understanding.

Objectives

1. To develop an understanding of the law of supply and demand.
2. To develop an understanding of how supply and demand affect prices.
3. To appreciate, understand and accept change.
4. To develop the ability to predict outcomes when certain facts or conditions are known.
5. To develop the ability to make and interpret graphs.

Initiating the Unit—Motivational Activities

■ Bring pictures to class which are representative of high priced items, moderately priced items, low priced items, and luxury items. Making no mention of these groupings, have youngsters suggest possible categories. Ask them on what basis they are making these decisions. Accept their suggestions and allow them to set up some sort of display. Set this aside and keep for reference later in the unit.

■ Set up situations where children may exchange services. Ask them to provide additional examples. Discuss what they are doing.

■ Bring in a few inexpensive items, pad of paper, pencils, erasers, crayons, etc., and offer to trade with the class. What do they offer in exchange? On what basis do they arrive at their conclusions?

■ Discuss setting up a "trading post." How would the youngsters go about it? How would they set prices? How would they attract customers? What would they have to know about "supply and demand"?

Developing the Unit—Informational Activities

Problem: What is meant by supply?

Generalization: Supply is the amount of goods that sellers will offer at all possible prices.

Content:

► Supply is that portion of goods and services which is offered for sale, and will be sold at all existing prices. (Amount of goods actually offered for sale.)

► Supply is affected by

1. number of persons desiring or needing the goods or services.
2. the ability of persons to pay for the goods or services.
3. the willingness of persons to pay a certain amount for the goods or services.

► When articles or services are in short supply, prices go up. If the supply exceeds the demand, prices go down.

► Other factors which influence supply are

1. production
2. availability of money
3. demand
4. add to list

Informational Activities

- Compile lists of articles that are in plentiful supply. Determine current prices for these articles. What generalizations can be made from the findings? What other factors might explain the prices of certain articles?
- Invite a local grocer or fruit dealer to speak to the class about the relationship between supply and price of his goods, including such influences as weather, season, etc.
- Have youngsters act out situations involving
    1. goods in short supply
    2. services in short supply
    3. goods in plentiful supply
    4. services in plentiful supply
    5. dealer withholding his supply
    6. several dealers involved in each of the above situations.

- Film (For the teacher)—*Law of Supply and Demand*—Coronet Films—Teacher may decide to show the film to the class if the class is able to understand the material.
- Develop a vocabulary list, include definitions.

Problem: What is meant by demand?

Generalization: Demand is the amount of goods or services that buyers are willing to take at any price.

Content:

► Demand is determined by several factors.
    1. The *needs* of the people.
    2. The *wants* of the people.
    3. The willingness of the people to pay a given price.
    4. The ability of the people to pay that price.

► Demand is related to supply. In fact, in some instances it determines the supply.
► Both demand and supply are factors which influence the price of goods and services.

Informational Activities

- Compile lists of articles that are currently in demand. Determine prices for these articles. What generalizations can be made from these findings? What other factors might explain the prices of certain articles? How do these findings compare with those arrived at while investigating *supply?*
- Invite a local merchant (dry goods, hardware or drug store) to speak to the group about how supply and demand affects his business. Include such things as markdowns, markups, sales, buying new merchandise, etc.
- Have youngsters form groups. Have each group decide a way in which they can demonstrate the law of supply and demand.
- Continue to add to the vocabulary list.

Problem: What is meant by equilibrium price?

Generalization: Equilibrium price is the price at which sellers can sell all they wish and buyers can buy all they wish.

Content:

- ▶ The forces of supply and demand move prices and available quantity towards an *equilibrium* or *balance.*
- ▶ When these forces are allowed to change, the public is benefited. This takes place in our free enterprise system.
- ▶ Discuss our free enterprise system.

Informational Activities

- Have youngsters develop graphs showing the
    1. demand for an article   2. supply of an article
- Now reproduce both graphs into transparencies (overlay). The point at which the supply curve and the demand curve intersect is the equilibrium price.
- Have youngsters visit the area high school bookstore. Have the manager give examples of equilibrium prices on certain books.
- Have children list the benefits of our free enterprise system. One chart can be devoted to the buyer, one to the seller.

- Have youngsters form groups of buyers and groups of sellers. Give buyers play money and sellers articles to sell. Have them use the principles they have learned in order to establish an equilibrium price.

Problem: How does price guide production?

Generalization: The price at which an item can be sold will influence production.

Content: Production is influenced by the price at which an article can be sold.

► If buyers cannot or will not pay the seller's price, the production of that item will slow down.
► If the article sells rapidly at a given price, the production will probably rise.
► Other related factors which influence production

1. Raw materials   3. Available labor
2. Wages   4. Utility
            5. Add to list

Informational Activities

- Have youngsters change roles from the last group activity. (The sellers will become the *consumers* and the buyers will become *producers.*) Set up situations that will exemplify the principles learned. Have prices determine the amount of goods that producers will manufacture.
- Have interested youngsters give a report on how this concept might affect the stock market.
- Have interested students research and report on what effects this concept has on the gross national product.

Problem: How does price guide consumption?

Generalization: The price at which an item can be sold influences consumption.

Content:

► Consumption is influenced by the price at which an article can be sold.

► It is also influenced by the amount of money people have to spend.

► Other factors which influence consumption

1. Utility	3. Status
2. Availability	4. Advertising
5. Add to list	

Informational Activities

• Groups may again change roles from the preceding activity. Set up situations that will point out the relationships between price and consumption.

• Have youngsters develop advertisements or commercials which will attract consumers. Have them use "price" in their appeal. Use both low priced and high priced goods.

• Examine newspaper and magazine ads to determine the types of appeals made to consumers.

Culminating the Unit—Summarizing Activities

■ Have the class plan to put on a play. Pretend that it is intended for a paying audience. What are some of the things that will have to be paid for? What will the total cost of the production be? Can some of the costs be reduced? If the production is going to show a profit, how much will the tickets have to be sold for? Will the public pay this price? If not, what will have to be done? Consider these and the many other questions which will arise.

■ Refer back to the pictures which were grouped by the youngsters at the outset of the unit. Ask them if there are any changes they would like to make now. Pictures should then be regrouped.

■ Have mimeographed sheets of problems which give youngsters certain market conditions. Have them *predict* the outcomes of these situations. Example: Roses are selling for $1.25 a dozen at the florist shop. Because of an upcoming event, roses are in great demand. In fact, the demand is greater than the supply. What can we reasonably predict for these known facts?

■ Hold a mock "auction." Have youngsters read about auctions, then write short histories about the articles up for bid. Have them determine prices of the articles to be sold, and attempt to determine the actual worth of the items. Have the children "bid" on items they want or need, and then pay for them with play money. Discuss the types of choices they made and how wisely (or foolishly) they spent their money.

■ Make arrangements to attend a real auction. Make a list of activities to watch for. This will give children an opportunity to see free competition in action.

Evaluation Techniques

Youngsters should be evaluated throughout the unit.
Observe youngsters to determine how well they make use of the information gathered in the unit.

Written Test on Information Gained in the Unit

DIRECTIONS: Fill in the missing word in the space provided. (Words may be put on the board if desired.)

1. The amount of goods that sellers will offer at all possible prices is called the *(supply)*.
2. If the article sells rapidly at a given price, the production will *(rise)*.
3. Both demand and supply are factors which influence the *(price)* of goods and services.
4. The price at which an item can be sold will influence *(production)* and *(consumption)*.
5. The amount of the goods or services that buyers are willing to take at any given price is called the *(demand)*.
6. If the supply exceeds the demand, prices go *(down)*.
7. If buyers cannot or will not pay the seller's price, the production of that item will *(slow down)*.
8. When articles or services are in short supply, prices go *(up)*.
9. *(Equilibrium price)* is the price at which sellers can sell all they wish and buyers can buy all they wish.
10. The forces of supply and demand move prices and available quantity towards an *(equilibrium or balance)*.

Problems using predicted outcomes may also be used as a part of the evaluation of the student's understanding.

SUPPLY AND DEMAND

References for Children

1. Chase, Stuart. *A Primer of Economics.* New York: Random House, 1944.
2. Foster, Constance J. *The Story of Money.* New York: Nedill, McBride Company, 1962.
3. Kane, Elmer R. *How Money and Credit Help Us.* Chicago: Benefic Press, 1966.

BANKS

This unit attempts to provide some answers to the many questions asked by children concerning banks. Three of the more important question are: "What is a bank?" "What kinds of banks are there?" and "How do banks do business?" Of course, the unit invites the student to go beyond these three questions. It introduces credit unions, labor banks and loan associations. The unit provides activities which will help the student gain insight into the federal reserve system, borrowing and saving, and various terms and concepts related to the banking business.

Make this unit an adventure into the world of banking. Provide the student an opportunity to capitalize on his interest in money, what it does, and where it goes. Examine the various occupations associated with the topic. Whatever the students' interests, they will discover worthwhile activities, interesting information, and maybe the beginnings of an "investment" in their future.

Objectives

1. To develop an understanding of the business of banking.
2. To develop an increasing appreciation of our entire economic system.
3. To develop computational and verbal skills and abilities.

Initiating the Unit—Motivational Activities

■ Arrange the room with pictures, objects, signs, so that it represents different sections of a bank. Example: Teller's cage, mortgage department, safety deposit section, loan section, etc.

■ Show and discuss a film on banking. (Teacher should preview films and decide if the level of the film is appropriate.)

> *Fred Meets a Bank*—11 minutes
>> Coronet Films
>
> *This Is Our Town: Banks, Investment, and Insurance*—10 minutes
>> Milwaukee Association of Commerce
>
> *Story of Money*—16 minutes
>> British Information Service
>
> *Using the Bank*—11 minutes
>> Encyclopaedia Britannica Films, Inc.

■ Have students select topics they might have to explore, such as,

1. the first bank
2. checking system
3. Federal Reserve System
4. important people in the banking field
5. add to list

■ Arrange with a bank to have students begin a savings account. Invite a bank official to class to discuss the procedure before students open their account.

■ Discuss with students the advantages and disadvantages of a savings account as compared with government bonds. As questions arise which they cannot answer, direct them to the books and other materials which you have set out around the room.

Developing the Unit—Informational Activities

Problem: What is a bank? Are there different kinds of banks?

Generalization: The most common type of bank is a commercial bank that deals in money and credit.

Content:

► A Bank

1. is a business
2. deals in money and credit
3. uses money to make loans and investments

► There are many different kinds of banks

1. commercial banks   4. trust companies
2. saving banks   5. credit unions
3. loan associations   6. labor banks
                    7. add to list

Informational Activities

• Have students get the definition of a bank from various sources. Each student is to ask someone (parent, principal, friend, uncle, real estate agent) for his definition of a bank. Have students discuss their findings and compare them to the dictionary's and encyclopedia's definition.
• Have the class organize into six committees. Each committee is to select a kind of bank to investigate and report on to the rest of the class. To do this, they must:
  1. prepare a poster about their bank,
  2. tell in a short story what the bank does,
  3. illustrate on the chalkboard how it differs from other kinds of banks,
  4. collect some pictures and articles about their type of bank.

• Have students write original poems and stories about banks.
• Ask students to bring in commercial games dealing with banking. *Example:* Monopoly
• Have a committee of students prepare an 8 mm. film clip on banks.
  1. Have students discuss what they should show in the film. *Examples:*
     a) Opening scene: Film introduction in block printing.
     b) A shot of the bank—outside—15 seconds

    c) The inside of the bank:

        president's office   vault

        teller's cage   security officers

                  depositors

2. Students should "map out" the film in terms of footage for each subject, lighting necessary, request to bank for filming, etc.

3. The entire class should evaluate the film.

Problem: What do banks do with the money people deposit?

Generalization: Banks use the money people deposit to make loans and investments.

Content:

▶ Banks are private businesses that:

1. accept deposits
2. invest deposits in terms of loans and investments
3. serve the needs of their investors and owners
4. keep some cash available
5. buy U.S. Government bonds
6. deal in credit with businesses, farmers, individuals, etc.

Informational Activities

- Ask a bank official to explain what his bank does with the money people deposit.
- Ask students to give examples of each of the following:

    1. deposit   3. loan

    2. depositor   4. credit

          5. investment

- Using play money establish a classroom bank. Have students deposit money in savings accounts for three days at 4½ per cent interest. (Each day can represent 1 year of deposit.) On the fourth day have each student request his money with the interest. What happens? Ask the students to discuss with the class why the bank ran out of money. Ask them why this does not happen in real banks.

- Have students do pencil sketches depicting what banks do. Arrange to show these paintings or sketches at the local banks.
- Select a committee of students to develop a "Picture History of Banks."
- Have another committee develop a picture book entitled "What Banks Do for You."

Problem: How do people borrow money from a bank? Why do people use a bank to save money?

Generalization: A bank is a private business that encourages people to save and borrow money.

Content:

► Loans

1. answer a need
2. collateral is needed
3. must arrange for payment
4. amount must be reasonable
5. interest charges on principal

► Checking Accounts

1. convenient
2. record of all payments
3. safe method

► Savings Account

1. open account with a small payment
2. 4½ per cent paid by bank on principal each year

► Mortgage

1. need collateral
2. need down payment
3. need employment

Informational Activities

- Ask a local bank to allow your class or a committee from the class to go through a mock procedure for borrowing money.

Establish a problem such as borrowing $100.00 for a class trip to Washington, D.C. Ask the bank for a loan.

- Have students ask their parents the advantages and disadvantages of having a checking or a savings account.
- Bring in samples of cancelled checks. Have students outline the transactions each check was involved in.
- Have pupils find out about various savings plans such as Christmas Clubs.
- Have students investigate the purpose, advantages, and obtain samples of the following checks:

  1. counter check   3. traveler's check
  2. cashier's check   4. certified check
                   5. money order

- Have a real estate agent explain the purposes of a mortgage and how one goes about getting a mortgage.
- Discuss with the class the meaning of words such as:

  1. collateral   3. principal
  2. down payment   4. rate
                   5. interest

- Have committees prepare bulletin board displays entitled:
  1. The Importance of Banks
  2. What Happens to the Check You Cash?
  3. How to Use a Bank

- Have students prepare a skit on banking for other classes. Some examples of titles are:
  1. Mr. Smith Buys a Home
  2. A Day in the Life of Mister Banker
  3. Why a Bank Spends What It Makes
  4. Sally's Christmas Club

Problem: What is the Federal Reserve System? How does it help the public?

Generalization: The Federal Reserve System is a regulating body for member banks.

Content:

► Federal Reserve System

1. established in 1913
2. prevents run on money
3. has 12 district banks, each having 24 branch banks
4. is supervised by a Board of Governors (7)
5. each Reserve bank has a nine member governing board
6. they regulate amount of currency and credit
7. less than half of all banks are members
8. all national banks must be members
9. members can borrow from the Federal Reserve Bank
10. adds to the stability of our economy

Informational Activities

• Invite a member of a Federal Reserve bank to talk to the class about the function and organization of the Federal Reserve System.
• Have students prepare a bulletin board display showing the relationship between Federal Reserve banks and their branch banks.
• Have a committee of students investigate the Federal Reserve Act of 1913 and tell why it was proposed.
• Have students discuss the advantages of belonging to the Federal Reserve System.
• Have three groups of students investigate:

1. Federal Reserve notes   3. commercial paper
2. bonds   4. gold certificates

• Have them report findings to the class.

Culminating the Unit—Summarizing Activities

■ Have the class prepare a filmstrip for use on the opaque projector. Have the students discuss what the filmstrip should contain, how long each sequence should be, and what kind of script will accompany the film.

■ Have the class prepare mimeographed booklets on various aspects of banking. For example, one booklet can be entitled,

"Banking Occupations." This booklet will tell the reader about the various occupations available in the banking business. Include sketches.

■ Invite parents to the final session of the unit on banking. Have students prepare a mock television presentation of what they have learned about banking. A type of behind the scenes presentation would be very effective. Provide time after the program for parents to question the students about their information and activities.

Evaluation Techniques

Youngsters should be evaluated throughout the unit.
Observe youngsters to determine how well they make use of the information gathered in the unit.

Written Test on Information Gained in the Unit

1. What is the Federal Reserve System? How does it help banks?
2. Describe what banks do with the money they receive from their depositors.
3. Sam went to the bank with $125.30 that he had saved. He asked the teller whether he should put it in a savings or a checking account. What would you advise him to do?
4. What are the differences between a savings bank and a credit union?
5. In what ways do people use banks? List as many ways as you can think of.
6. Identify the following in one or two sentences:
   (*a*) securities   (*e*) teller
   (*b*) Robert Morris   (*f*) collateral
   (*c*) debt   (*g*) promissory note
   (*d*) investment   (*h*) assets
7. Compute the interest on a savings account balance of $1,845.00. The interest paid is 4½ per cent compounded semiannually.
8. Why does a bank charge more interest on a loan than it pays on a savings account?

BANKS

References for Children

1. Elkin, Benjamin. *The True Book of Money*. Chicago: Children's Press, 1959.
2. Kane, Elmer. *How Money and Credit Help Us*. Chicago: Benefic Press, 1966.
3. Reinfeld, Fred. *Story of Paper Money*. New York: Sterling, 1957.
4. Ress, Elinor. *At the Bank*. Chicago: Melmont Publishers, 1959.
5. Russell, Solveig. *From Barter to Gold*. Chicago: Rand McNally and Company, 1961.
6. Sootin, Laura. *Let's Go to a Bank*. New York: G. P. Putnam's Sons, 1957.

SAVINGS, LOANS AND INTEREST

References for Children

1. Chase, Stuart. *A Primer of Economics*. New York: Random House, 1944.
2. Elkin, Benjamin. *The True Book of Money*. Chicago: Children's Press, 1960.
3. Foster, Constance. *The Story of Money*. New York: Nedill, McBride Company, 1962.
4. Ress, Elinor. *At The Bank*. Chicago: Melmont Publishers, 1959.
5. Russell, Solveig. *From Barter to Gold*. Chicago: Rand McNally Company, 1961.
6. Sootin, Laura. *Let's Go to a Bank*. New York: G. P. Putnam's Sons, 1957.

CREDIT

The study of credit can be most meaningful to all students. In our credit card era, it is important to understand the advantages and disadvantages of credit. The "buy now—pay later" philosophy demands that the consumer be watchful and cautious. Adequate knowledge of the credit system can help the student in his daily activities. This unit is particularly relevant then, as it helps prepare children for this great adventure in buying.

The word *credit* comes from the Latin word *credere*—to believe or trust. How much one can believe or trust another, determines his credit rating. Certainly something as important as this should be understood by our future citizens!

The student will also explore installment buying, mortgages, per cent and interest, and thrift. The activities in the unit will help link the knowledge of credit with the units on banking and taxes. Together they should provide students with meaningful concepts for future decisions.

Objectives

1. To help students understand the credit system operating in our economy.
2. To develop an appreciation of the advantages and disadvantages of credit buying.
3. To learn the skills and abilities necessary for effective evaluation of credit plans.

Initiating the Unit—Motivational Activities

■ Have a ten word spelling test each day. Instead of grading the tests after they are taken, provide each student with a credit rating, (number of words he will probably spell correctly). *Example:* seven points of credit, eight points of credit, etc. Thus, a student with a daily credit rating of seven is expected to spell seven out of ten words correctly each day. Provide each student with ten credit tickets. Each day he gets a credit check following the test. Everytime he goes under his credit rating he must return to the bank (a student) the number of credit tickets under his credit rating. Thus, a student with a credit rating of seven who spells five words correctly must return two credit tickets to the banker. If the student spells nine words correctly he receives two credit tickets. Every time a student spells ten words correctly, he receives five *bonus* credit tickets. The student with the most tickets wins the game.

■ Have students prepare an exhibit of items, pictures, newspaper and magazine articles relating to credit.

■ Invite an official of a credit union, department store, or local bank to discuss with the students
1. what credit is
2. what the advantages and disadvantages of credit are, and
3. what basic knowledge consumers should have about credit.

Problem: What is credit?

Generalization: Credit is a purchase made by someone who promises to pay later.

Content:

► Credit—Latin derivation meaning "to believe or trust."

Informational Activities

• Ask students what it means to "buy now—pay later," or "pay as you go."

Problem: How and why do people use credit?

Generalization: Individuals use credit because it enables them to have the goods before they are fully paid for.

Content:

► Credit is used in

1. manufacturing
2. commerce
3. transportation
4. agriculture
5. construction
6. family finances

► Credit ratings—the extent to which a man is considered trustworthy in meeting his financial obligations.

Informational Activities

• Have students conduct a survey of parents, business men, the principal, etc., to gather opinions on the uses of credit. Prepare a list of interview questions, such as:
1. Do you use credit?
2. Is it of value to you? Why?
3. Does your business use credits? Why?

- Select six committees to study how credit is used in each of the areas listed in the subject matter outline.
- Have students prepare a bulletin board displaying the uses of credit.
- Ask students to cite examples in their own lives where credit is used.
- Have students compare credit ratings to report card grades.

Problem: What kinds of credit plans do people use?

Generalization: Various credit plans are available, each with advantages and disadvantages.

Content:

► Kinds of credit

1. installment buying.
2. credit cards
3. contract plan
4. book credit

► Installment buying

1. may make a down payment
2. pay balance according to a plan—weekly, monthly, bi-annually
3. most real estate, automobiles, household appliances, etc. are bought on this plan
4. a charge is usually affixed to installment buying
   (*a*) carrying charge
   (*b*) interest rate on unpaid balance

► Credit cards
► Contract plan—mortgage—a contract or other evidence of the debt of the purchaser.
► Book credit—open accounts—such as a person charging food at a grocery store—grocer records items purchased.

Informational Activities

- Have students bring in advertisements that allow the purchaser the use of

1. credit cards
2. a contract
3. installment buying
4. book credit

- Using "play money," have students buy consumer goods on the installment plan.

  1. Select three or four students to serve as sellers of a product. Have them establish their own purchase plan. Let them set up a "desk store" to sell their merchandise.
  2. Let other class members buy the material of their choice from the four sellers.
  3. After students have practice in this area, ask the sellers to initiate plans for getting more customers.

- Have students start a "credit card hunt." In one week they are to find as many different kinds of credit cards as possible. They should not bring the credit cards to school, but they should list the company and its products or services—gasoline, tires, car repairs, and so on.
- Ask the students for their views on what a mortgage is. Use a monopoly game to introduce and teach these concepts.
- Ask a real estate agent to explain to the class how a person obtains a mortgage.
- Ask the students to find examples of book credit. (This was once popular, but is slowly being replaced by other forms of credit.)

Problem: What are the advantages and disadvantages of credit buying?

Generalization: Buying on time has both advantages and disadvantages.

Content:

► Advantages

  1. obtain product without cash
  2. use product immediately
  3. keeps the economy stable
     (*a*) production   (*b*) employment

► Disadvantages

  1. may be used excessively
  2. people may buy unwisely
  3. may lead to greater debt

► Thrift

1. wise use of money   2. budget plans

Informational Activities

• Prepare an overhead transparency on buying an automobile or a television set. *Example:*

```
┌──────────────────────────────────────────────┐
│                                                │
│          BUY  A  COLOR  TV  SET                │
│                                                │
│                                                │
│                              CASH PRICE        │
│                                 $520           │
│                                                │
│  NO MONEY DOWN                                 │
│                                                │
│        SMALL INTEREST RATE                     │
│        1 % on unpaid balance                   │
│        Up to 12 months to pay                  │
│                                                │
└──────────────────────────────────────────────┘
```

Figure 7-1

• *Ask:*

1. How many think that the company is giving you a chance to buy this TV set with money?
2. What does "small interest charge per month on unpaid balance" mean?
3. How much does the set cost? How much will it cost if you made the following payments (remember to add the interest each month): January $50.; February $100.; March $200.; April $100.00; May—paid the entire unpaid balance. ($536.45 is the total cost. May payment is $86.45.)
4. What are the advantages to paying for the television set as soon as possible?
5. What are the disadvantages of taking the entire twelve months to pay for the set?

• Tell students that we can buy an item (car, refrigerator, etc.) by paying the seller cash for it. We will get the money from a bank or a loan association. The special words used to record these transactions are:

1. principal—amount borrowed
2. interest—money paid for the money borrowed
3. rate—per cent charged as interest

- Have each class member select an item he would like to buy. Using "play money" have two students serve as bankers and two as loan association presidents. The bankers are to charge an interest of 4½ per cent, the loan association officers are to charge 6 per cent on the principal. Have students determine the total cost of their item if they obtain a loan from the bank and compare it to the cost if they obtain the loan from the loan association.
- Have students examine a gasoline station credit card to determine whether or not an interest charge is required. If so, how much is it? Under what conditions will interest be charged?
- Ask an automobile dealer to "sell" the class a car and go through the procedure an actual purchaser must experience. How much does the car actually cost? What is the down payment? What is the cost of the license? What about a registration fee, etc.? What is the actual fee paid by the purchaser once he agrees to accept the car?
- Have each student select an advertisement from a magazine or newspaper that shows something he can buy. Look for ads that indicate interest rates, payment plans, etc. Ask each student to determine the cost of the item if he bought it for cash or on a monthly plan. Which does he prefer? Why?
- Have students write a story or a play on the uses and abuses of credit. Some students might prefer a puppet show to dramatize the topic.
- Send a committee of students to the library for books, stories, and articles on the topics of credit, savings, or some other related area. Have the committee bring these books back to the class for students to read. Give each student a credit card (Figure 7-2). Have two students serve as "bankers." Their job is to punch the number of books read by students in the

class. When a student has read 20 books, he receives a special credit rating card with an A on it; 15 books obtains a B; etc.

- Ask students what is meant by thrift? Ask: "What is a budget?" Have students give examples of budgeting. Relate the budgeting of money to the budgeting of time. Ask: "Do you budget your time? Why? How is this related to a budgeting of money?"

```
1 2,0 19 18 17 16 15
2                14     NAME_____
3   READING      13
4                12     GRADE _____
5 6  7  8  9  10 11
```

Figure 7-2

- Have students make out a weekly time budget plan. After it has been completed, ask: "How much time do you spend reading? Watching television? Playing?"
- Discuss with the class the question: "Should people have everything they want?" List the pros and cons on the board.

1. What determines whether people can buy what they desire? (income, family size, price, taste, need, etc.)
2. It has been said that "money is the root of all evil." Discuss this statement.
3. How are income and spending related?

```
        CREDIT RATING

        _____

NAME _____
```

Figure 7-3

- Have the class prepare a school poster contest on the topic of thrift. Ask the class to select five judges; two classmates and three adults from the school or the P.T.A. Establish committees to develop entrance rules, displaying of the posters, etc.

Problem: What is bankruptcy?

Generalization: Bankruptcy is a legal means of helping an individual or business that cannot pay debts.

Content:

► The bankrupt

1. cannot pay debts
2. files a petition of bankruptcy
3. does not have to pay debts if petition is granted
4. a trustee (appointed by the court) takes possession of assets
5. trustee sells assets and pays creditors in proportion to their share of the total debt.

Informational Activities

- Have a lawyer explain the meaning and implications of bankruptcy.
- Ask a committee of students to trace the history of bankruptcy. When did it first appear in this country? What was its purpose? Have them report their findings to the class.
- Have class groups interview people for their ideas on bankruptcy. For example, do the people interviewed know what bankruptcy means? What misconceptions do they have? Prepare an interview sheet before students start their investigation.
- Have class groups prepare skits on bankruptcy. Have other members of the class point out how bankruptcy might have been avoided in each case.

Culminating the Unit—Summarizing Activities

■ Have the class prepare a radio play on the topic of credit. It should be documentary in nature, perhaps directed to the housewife.

■ Have each student prepare a short report on the learnings they have acquired during this unit. Have them prepare the report based on the following questions:

1. What is credit?
2. What do you now know about credit that you did not know before?
3. How has this unit on credit helped you in better understanding our economic system?

■ Have students arrange a debate for other classes on the issue: Resolved: It is wiser to pay cash than to buy on credit.
■ Show the films:

Installment Buying—Coronet Films—10 minutes
What Is a Contract?—Coronet Films—10 minutes
Your Thrift Habits—Coronet Films—11 minutes

■ Have students start a ledger showing their expenditures. They should keep in mind the concepts of budgeting presented. This ledger should be referred to periodically as the semester progresses.

Evaluation Techniques

Youngsters should be evaluated throughout the unit.
Observe youngsters to determine how well they make use of the information gathered in the unit.

Written Test on Information Gained in the Unit

1. If you wished to buy a house, you probably would have to obtain a mortgage. What is a mortgage?
2. What is a credit rating?
3. Give an example of installment buying.
4. What are the advantages and disadvantages of credit cards?

5. What is a budget? Describe some of the advantages of budgeting.
6. Give an example of the following:
   (*a*) principal (*b*) interest (*c*) carrying charge
7. Do you think there should be credit cards for children? For example, the card might be used for admission to movies, for buying books, for buying candy, etc. What would be the advantages? Disadvantages?
8. Your father buys a $1300 automobile. Because he does not have that much cash, he trades in the old car for $300 and adds $200 in cash to the down payment. The finance company gives him 20 months to pay the balance. In paying the balance over a period of 20 months, your father must pay the finance company one per cent interest a month on the unpaid balance. Thus, for 20 months he must pay $40 plus one per cent of the remaining unpaid balance. How much does your father eventually pay for the car that originally cost $1300?
9. Explain what is meant by the term bankruptcy.
10. Develop a rule for the wise use of buying with credit.

CREDIT

References for Children

1. Chase, Stuart. *A Primer of Economics*. New York: Random House, 1944.
2. Foster, Constance. *The Story of Money*. New York: Nedill, McBride and Company, 1962.
3. Kane, Elmer. *How Money and Credit Help Us*. New York: The Macmillan Co., 1966.

References for Teachers

1. Cassell, Francis. *Gold and Credit*. New York: Frederick Praeger, 1965.
2. Gemmill, Paul. *Current Introductory Economics*. New York: Harper and Brothers, 1955.
3. Harwood, Edward. *Causes and Control of the Business Cycle*. Great Barrington, Mass.: American Institute for Economics, 1957.

TAXES

Although much is said about taxes in sarcasm and humor, they are important. Through taxes we are provided numerous services, protections and benefits. In this unit, we try to provide a cross section of various tax methods that will help you and your students appreciate the breadth of the tax base. The tax base is of three principal types—the income tax, the property tax, and the sales tax. From these three kinds of taxes, students can discover the means for assessing and collecting these taxes. Discussion and investigation of the withholding tax plan, the income tax forms, sales taxes, poll taxes, inheritance taxes and the like, will prove informative and interesting.

The activities in this unit will provide insights into the importance of our tax system, federal, state, and local budgets, and the problems of receipts and expenditures.

Objectives

1. To develop an appreciation and understanding of our tax system.
2. To develop an understanding of the kinds of taxes used to support our government and how these taxes provide benefits to our citizens.
3. To enable the student to effectively utilize the knowledge he receives in order to solve problems and create ideas.

Initiating the Unit—Motivational Activities

▪ Have each student interview three adults on the topic of taxes. Have each student use the following questions in the interview:

1. How do you feel about taxes?
2. What taxes do you pay?
3. What services do your taxes provide?

▪ Follow this activity with a discussion period for an analysis and synthesis of the comments students receive. What conclusions can students come to as a result of the interviews?

■ On individual index cards, write a problem based on the information provided in the unit. For example, on one card write property tax, on another sales tax, then poll tax, estate tax, tariffs, social security tax, etc. Have each student research any aspect of the problem that he wishes, and report his findings to the class.

■ Provide each student with two hundred dollars worth of "play money." Each day for one week provide situations in which certain students will have to pay classroom taxes. Have students elect an assessor and a tax collector.

> *Sample situation 1:* For this week only, students will have to pay a poll tax of $1.00 for every situation in which the class takes a vote.
>
> *Sample situation 2:* For this week only, students who take the school bus will have to pay a franchise tax of 25¢ per day.
>
> *Sample situation 3:* For this week only, students who use school rulers or paper must pay a tariff of 15¢ each time the ruler is used and 10¢ per piece of paper.

■ As the situations arise, the teacher can explain the type of tax and make arrangements with the tax assessor and collector to keep records of the money paid and collected.

Developing the Unit—Informational Activities

Problems: What are taxes? Why do we need them?

Generalization: People pay money to the government in order that it may carry out certain functions.

Content:

► Taxes
1. are used by the government to provide services
2. are levied by
   a) federal government
   b) state government
   c) local government

Informational Activities

- Have the class prepare a letter requesting student handbooks and a teacher's manual entitled *Teaching Taxes,* Internal Revenue Service, Washington, D.C. (Teacher's signature is required.) Ask for classroom quantities.
- Encourage students to find out why there are federal, state, and local taxes.
- Have certain students give oral reports on taxes that people did not agree with such as the Stamp Act, the tax on tea (Boston Tea Party), etc.
- Have students prepare a hand puppet show depicting taxes of long ago. For example, how did the Egyptians or societies living under the feudal system get tax money? Were the pyramids built with tax money?
- Students can use hand puppets to tell the story of the Stamp Act, Boston Tea Party, etc.
- Have selected students use a tape recorder to record interviews with various resource people.
- Have students prepare short plays concerning taxes. Emphasis should be placed on what they are and why they are necessary.

Problem: What kinds of taxes do people pay?

Generalization: Government is supported and operated by a variety of tax collections.

Content:

► Kinds of taxes

1. property		6. estate	
2. income		7. excise	
3. sales		8. tariff	
4. corporation		9. license	
5. inheritance		10. franchise	
	11. severance		

Informational Activities

- Each student should be encouraged to bring in for a bulletin board display, one newspaper article on some kind of tax or tax problem.
- Have each student use reference books to find the difference in each kind of tax listed in the subject matter outline.
- Select a committee to find out what the federal and state taxes are on gasoline, tobacco, liquor, and entertainment. Discuss why these items are taxed.
- Select certain students to find out what the tobacco salesman or the garage man does with the federal and state taxes he collects.
- Have some students write to local tax authorities requesting information about their jobs.
- Have students look up various agencies in the telephone book. Have them record the various city and state agencies that serve the people such as building inspection, agricultural agencies, recreation department, conservation department, police department, etc. What role do taxes play in supporting these functions?
- Invite various persons from the above agencies to discuss the problems of taxation.
- Have the superintendent or someone designated by him discuss with the class how schools are supported and what monies are used.
- Ask students if they recall their parents paying a toll bridge tax or turnpike tax. Discuss the reasons for these taxes.
- Develop arithmetic problems using different taxes as the central theme for all problems. *Example:*
    1. If the sales tax on a pound of butter was 3¢, what would the tax be on 5 pounds?
    2. John's father spent 32¢ for each gallon of gasoline he put in his car. Of this, 10¢ was the federal tax, 3¢ was the state share. He has an automobile that uses 300 gallons of gasoline per year. What was the total tax John's father had to pay last year on the gasoline he used? What was the total federal tax? Total state tax?

Problem: What does the government do with the money collected by taxation?

Generalization: Money collected by the government provides services for the people.

Content:

► Federal Budget

   1. Receipts—taxes
   2. Expenditures

(*a*) defense	(*f*) transportation
(*b*) welfare	(*g*) natural resources
(*c*) benefits	(*h*) education
(*d*) research	(*i*) salaries
(*e*) commerce	(*j*) add to list

► State and Local Budgets

   1. Receipts—taxes
   2. Expenditures

(*a*) police departments	(*e*) health departments
(*b*) schools	(*f*) libraries
(*c*) fire departments	(*g*) streets and roads
(*d*) garbage collection and disposal	(*h*) add to list

Informational Activities

• Have students record on a calendar their receipts and expenditures each day for one month. How would this help them at tax time?
• Have students investigate the various taxes that federal, state and local governments collect. *Example:*

   1. Income taxes
   2. Corporation taxes
   3. Excise taxes

• Using graphs of various types, prepare a bulletin board display showing what the government does with the tax money it collects.

- Much of the state and local revenue comes from a property tax. Invite the local assessor to discuss with the students the advantages and disadvantages of the property tax.
- Have a group of students go to the next town meeting. Ask them to discuss attendance, agenda, procedure, etc. (This would also be a good experience for the entire class.)
- Invite some of the following resource people to discuss taxes with the class:
    1. an agent of the Internal Revenue Service
    2. a Treasury Department agent
    3. the local tax collector
    4. a customs officer
    5. the state treasurer or a representative

- Tell the class that collectively they will become the local government. Have them elect a mayor and other city officials. Every student should have a position. Have the mayor call a meeting to discuss the budget. Have each student prepare his budget request and state reasons for the money requested. Have the tax assessor determine the amount of income that can be expected. Use newspaper articles on the local budget to help the class prepare the budget. Provide problems for the mayor to discuss at the budget meeting. *Example:* How can we keep taxes at a minimum yet provide adequate services to the citizens?
- Students can make hand puppets to illustrate various kinds of taxes. For example, a hand puppet can be made to illustrate the inheritance tax. The student responsible for this would prepare his script and through his puppet, tell the class about the inheritance tax.

Problem: What is the income tax?

Generalization: Most of the federal government monies come from individual taxes.

Content:

► Individual Income Tax

1. purpose of	3. withholding tax
2. method of collecting	4. forms used

► Withholding

1. certificates used
2. purpose of
   (*a*) pay as you go
   (*b*) prevents problems of one large payment at the end
   of the year

Informational Activities

• Have each student discuss the income tax with his parents
  and relate to the class the results of the discussion.
• Write to the Internal Revenue Service (local office) for
  sample copies of Form 1040 and 1040A.
• Distribute to each student a withholding certificate (Form
  1040—1040A). Read the certificate with the class, asking
  them to explain each of the six categories on the certificate.
  Have students discuss why the withholding idea is good for
  the employer.

    Patsloff, Patricia. *Who Me? Teach Income Tax? Education
    Age.* Minnesota Mining and Manufacturing Co., Jan.–Feb.
    1966.

• Have students study these forms. If possible, have each
  student complete the form after determining a fictitious
  salary for the year.
• Have students use their withholding certificate to determine
  a fictitious sum of money that has been withheld.
• Assist students in using the tax table that comes with the
  1040A forms.
• Have students investigate the meaning of some of the following terms:

    1. joint return   4. contributions
    2. deductions   5. exemptions
    3. gross income   6. dependents

• Have students prepare a "learning tape" on taxes.
• A roller box movie can be prepared by some pupils to dramatize what happens when one does not pay his taxes. Have a

group of youngsters research this topic and present their "movie" to other members of the class.

Culminating the Unit—Summarizing Activities

■ Have students prepare a fact sheet on each of the following taxes:

1. custom duties
2. excise tax
3. gasoline tax
4. inheritance tax

5. license tax
6. property tax
7. sales tax
8. income tax

■ Have students prepare a dramatization of the Boston Tea Party.
■ Have a committee of students prepare charts and graphs of the services that tax supported agencies provide the people. For example, at the federal level, committees can prepare material on the expenditures for national defense, agriculture, health–education–welfare, veterans benefits and services, space research, and so on.
■ Prepare an exhibit for other students and teachers displaying all of the material used during the unit. Have each student explain what each item is used for, and how it relates to taxes.
■ Show the film:

Federal Taxation—10 minutes, Coronet Films

Evaluation Techniques

Youngsters should be evaluated throughout the unit.
Observe youngsters to determine how well they make use of the information gathered in the unit.

Written Test on Information Gained in the Unit

1. In what ways do taxes help us?
2. There are numerous kinds of taxes. Select five and tell how each is different from other taxes.
3. As a taxpayer, it will be necessary for you to complete a W 2 Form–Withholding Statement. Why is this necessary?

4. One Saturday morning, Cliff went with his father to buy some things. The list below tells some of the things Cliff's father did. After each of the items, tell what kind of tax Cliff's father had to pay.

ITEM	KIND OF TAX
Bought gasoline	(sales)
Registered the dog	(license)
Bought pipe tobacco	(sales)
Paid a fee for land he received when his father died	(inheritance)
Bought groceries	(sales)

5. What is the difference between receipts and expenditures?

6. In what ways are local monies used to help you and your family?

7. Should everyone pay the same percentage of taxes? Why or why not?

8. Some economists say that the land tax (property) is out of date. Do you agree or disagree with this statement? Support your answer.

9. Some people have suggested that citizens pay an "air tax" just as we pay for the the water we use, or the roads we drive on. How do you feel about this suggestion? Would you support legislation of this type? Why? Why not?

10. Identify in one or two sentences each of the following:
 (*a*) tariff   (*c*) Boston Tea Party
 (*b*) assessor   (*d*) tithe
           (*e*) tax rate

TAXES

References for Children

1. Chase, Stuart. *A Primer of Economics*. New York: Random House, 1944.
2. Disraeli, Robert. *Uncle Sam's Treasury*. New York: Random House, 1951.

3. Foster, Constance. *The Story of Money*. New York: Nedill, Mc-Bride Company, 1962.
4. Kane, Elmer. *How Money and Credit Help Us*. Chicago: Benefic Press, 1966.

ECONOMICS

References for Teachers

The following books contain excellent information on banks, savings, loans, interest, taxes, and supply and demand.

1. Chandler, Lester. *A Preface to Economics*. New York: Harper and Row Publishers, 1947.
2. Gemmill, Paul. *Current Introductory Economics*. New York: Harper and Row Publishers, 1955.
3. Gemmill, Paul. *Fundamentals of Economics*. New York: Harper and Row Publishers, 1960.
4. Hicks, J. P., Hart, A. G., and Ford, James. *Social Framework of the American Economy*. New York: Oxford University Press, 1955.
5. Joint Council of Economic Education. Washington, D.C. Write for list of available materials.
6. Michelon, L. C. *Basic Economics*. New York: World Publishing Company, 1960.
7. Paton, William. *Shirtsleeve Economics*. New York: Appleton-Century-Crofts, Inc., 1957.
8. Samuelson, Paul. *Economics: An Introductory Analysis*. New York: McGraw-Hill Book Co., 1964.
9. Soule, George. *Economics for Living*. New York: Abelard-Schuman, 1961.

Chapter 8

Exploring the New Frontiers: Outer Space and Oceanography

Predictions that man would someday live on the moon or in the depths of the sea once made excellent science fiction stories. However, the fiction is becoming a reality. This chapter deals with the realm of man's exploration from the darkness below the sea's surface, to the darkness of outer space. Wherever he goes, man is guided by his intelligence, his imagination, and certain scientific principles.

The first unit—Space Exploration—establishes the scientific principles that determine the "rules and regulations" of space travel. The concepts of gravity, inertia, centrifugal force are developed via the fascinating study of space travel. Questions such as: What is space? Why are rockets used? How does a satellite stay in orbit? provide the framework for meaningful learning experiences for your students.

The second unit—Project Apollo—utilizes the science concepts of the first unit to explain man's most ambitious space venture to date. Student excitement will be reflected in their eagerness to determine just how man will live on the moon. Their interest and questions will lead to further study of many new concepts of aerospace science.

What about the astronauts themselves? What training is necessary to become an astronaut? How does it feel to be an astro-

156

naut? What is it like to live as an astronaut? Are there any job possibilities in this area? These and many other questions will be explored in the third unit of this chapter—Astronauts.

The final unit—Oceanography—lets you and your students explore the newest of the sciences. Probing the secrets of the sea will truly be an adventure for your class. Going down into the sea with the aquanauts in Sealab II will spark the imagination and nourish the curiosity of your students.

As research progresses and new techniques for space and sea exploration are developed, your students will be more knowledgeable and have a greater appreciation of things to come. The concepts and problems in this chapter will have helped them move toward this objective.

SPACE EXPLORATION

This unit should precede the units titled *Project Apollo* and *Astronauts*. A study of space exploration demands some knowledge of basic scientific principles. Basic concepts have been selected that should help your class appreciate and understand that the universe is orderly and suitable for scientific investigation and prediction. Children are also exposed to many misconceptions about space. Effective use of this unit may help correct these misconceptions.

Objectives

1. To develop an understanding of scientific principles related to space travel.
2. To develop an appreciation of the vast amount of knowledge needed by man to successfully travel in space.
3. To develop skills in scientific investigation and procedures.
4. To promote an interest in science as a possibility for a future career or a leisure-time activity.

Initiating the Unit—Motivational Activities

■ Show a film on space travel. Have students make note of the vehicles used; the equipment and supplies needed; and the problems encountered. Good films for this purpose are:

> *A Trip to the Moon*—16 minutes
> Encyclopaedia Britannica Films, Inc.
> *First Men into Space*—16 minutes
> Encyclopaedia Britannica Films, Inc.
> *Reaching into Space*—14 minutes
> International Film Bureau
> *Exploring the Moon*—16 minutes
> McGraw-Hill Text-Films

> (Check with your nearest film rental library to secure these and other films and filmstrips mentioned.)

■ Prepare a chart (2' x 4') similar to the one in Figure 8-1.

DEFINITION BY	CLASS	TEXTBOOK	NEWSPAPER	MAGAZINE
SPACE				
METEORITE				
GRAVITY				
ACCELERATION				
ETC.				

Figure 8-1

■ Stress vocabulary development. Encourage the youngsters to use new words as they are encountered. Using the team approach, have students quiz each other.

Developing the Unit—Informational Activities

Problem: What is space?

Generalization: Space is beyond the atmosphere. It is endless, cold, dark, and airless.

Content:

► In order to understand the characteristics of outer space, students should have some concepts concerning our atmosphere.

► Students should understand that

1. our galaxy is one of billions of galaxies in the universe.
2. the atmosphere which envelops our entire earth, extends more than 100 miles upward.

Informational Activities

• Discuss with students what one finds in space. *Example:* In the universe we find planets, stars, meteors, etc.
• Discuss life on other planets. What are the possibilities? Have a committee of students research this topic and report to the class.

   Filmstrip—*Life on Other Planets*—Eyegate House

• Discuss the following questions:

1. Where does outer space begin? (Generally accepted definition is: "Where the atmosphere appears to end.")
2. What is the difference between outer space and the atmosphere? List student answers.

SPACE	*ATMOSPHERE*
no air	air
no pressure	pressure
dark	light and dark
endless	not endless
cold	temperature varies

3. How do planets stay in space? Why don't they collide? Why don't they burn up near the sun?

• Have students discuss these questions in class. Tape record their answers. Have each student verify some of the hypotheses stated using reference material from space books, textbooks, encyclopedias and the like.

- There are certain words used in "space talk" that must be defined and understood. *Examples:*

  Satellite: Discuss the meanings of this word with the class. What is a *satellite?* Poland is said to be a Russian *satellite.* The U.S. sends communication *satellites* into orbit around the earth. The moon is an earth *satellite.*

  Orbit: Youngsters will probably give a definition similar to "something that goes around something else." Be particularly concerned with the word *around.* Youngsters think of *orbit* as circular when in space flight it is actually elliptical.

- Other words to define include:

perigee	retro-rockets
apogee	thrust
combustion	inertia
extra-vehicular	astronaut
weightlessness	heat shield
acceleration	rendezvous
g-force	payload
burnout	docking

- Show the film or filmstrip *What Is Space?* Have a discussion prior to showing. A detailed follow-up is important.

  Film—*What Is Space?* Encyclopaedia Britannica Films, Inc.

  Filmstrip—*What Is Space?* Jam Handy Organization

Problem: Why are rockets used for space travel?

Generalization: Machines are used to overcome the gravitational attraction of the earth.

Content:

► Discussion about machines that help us to overcome gravity.

► Any machine that burns fuel to produce energy must have a source of oxygen.

▶ For fuel to burn in space where there is no oxygen, an engine must take along its own supply.

▶ Rockets are used for space travel because they carry their own fuel supply.

▶ The "step principle" of rocketry is used for sending "pay-loads" into space.

Informational Activities

• Develop a chart concerning machines and the source of energy that they use to overcome gravity.

• To develop the idea that oxygen is necessary for burning, use the following experiment:

• Place three candles on a table or desk. Light each candle. Have three students carefully place a glass over each candle at the same time, as shown in Figure 8-2.

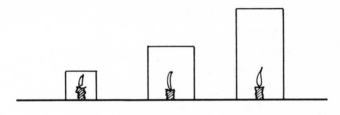

Figure 8-2

• Ask the class: Which candle went out first? Why? What makes the candles burn and then go out when the glasses are placed over them? Lead the class to the understanding that oxygen (gas/air) is necessary for combustion (burning). Repeat the experiment using three different students. Indicate that it is combustion that causes the energy that makes engines work for us. How does this apply to an engine as it approaches the outer limits of the atmosphere? (The fuel would have no oxygen with which to combine and therefore could not burn.)

• Introduce students to rocket terminology, such as: launch vehicle, piggyback booster, solid fuel, etc. Have students continue to develop their space dictionary.

- Have the class discuss the differences between jet engines and rockets.

  1. Why are rockets used for space travel instead of jet engines?
  2. What is the "building block" idea used by space engineers?

- Using three toy windup cars, illustrate the "step principle" of rocketry. First, line up the three cars side by side. Let them go and then measure the distance traveled by each one. Second, let one car go. At the point where it stops, start the second car. Use the same procedure for the third. Now measure the total distance traveled. Draw conclusions.
- Space notebook. Each student should be encouraged to keep a scrapbook on space travel. Include pictures of various rockets. Each picture should be followed by descriptions of the rocket, its stages, thrust, height, etc.
- Using a diagram from a text, have students explain how a rocket engine works. (Fuel and oxygen combine, burn in the combustion chamber and cause tremendous pressure on the front well of the rocket, causing it to move.)
- Have students use hydrogen peroxide and baking soda to demonstrate that it is possible to make oxygen.
- Show the film—

  Rockets: How They Work—16 minutes.
  Encyclopaedia Britannica Films, Inc.

Problem: In what direction, and to what extent does the earth's gravity pull on various objects?

Generalization: All objects are pulled toward the earth's center. Weight is a measure of gravity's pull.

Content:

► Discuss what gravity is and what it does.
► Develop the idea that the weight of an object is a measure of the earth's pull on that object.

► Distinguish between weight and mass.
► Develop the idea that gravity attracts all objects toward the center of the Earth.

Informational Activities

• Provide books that contain information about gravity for pupils to read. Have interested pupils give a report on Isaac Newton.
• Have pupils weigh a variety of articles to measure the earth's pull on these objects.
• Have pupils distinguish between weight and mass by weighing different articles and comparing their relative sizes. What relationships exist?
• Suspend a string so that it will swing freely. Children should swing it several times and mark the spot where it comes to rest.

> In what direction is gravity pulling? (Straight down)
> What would happen if the string was on the other side of the earth? (Same observation)

• Attach cardboard figures to a world globe. Determine the direction of the pull of gravity if a ball were being dropped by the figures.
• Art work. Draw pictures showing what might take place if gravity ceased to work.
• Language arts—creative writing. Describe what would happen if, for one day, there would be no gravity in your town.

Problem: How does speed help in space travel? How does a rocket keep from falling back to earth?

Generalization: Speed counteracts gravity.

Content:

► Develop the idea that man must develop machines for space travel that will overcome the force of gravity. Thus, they use tremendous rockets (some are 22 stories high) to overcome the earth's gravitational pull.

► Inertia may be defined as follows: A body at rest tends to remain at rest and a body in motion tends to remain in motion unless some force acts upon it.

► A satellite (moon, Earth, man-made) remains in orbit because gravity and centrifugal force achieve a balance. In other words, the inward pull of gravity is balanced by the outward push of centrifugal force. Speed helps to establish centrifugal force.

Informational Activities

• Discuss with the class why huge rockets are used for space travel. What do the rockets do?

• *Ask the class:* What happens when a driver of a car steps on the accelerator? (Speed is increased; we sometimes feel our bodies pushed against the seat.) Ask: When a driver makes his car go faster, what word can we use to describe this? (Speed–motion–acceleration). Relate the word acceleration to the accelerator in the car. Thus, help the class arrive at the definition that acceleration is "increase in speed."

• Have the class relate the word "acceleration" to the word "movement." When something is moved at the same speed we need something to stop it or slow it down. This is related to *inertia*. Put the word *inertia* on the board.

• Demonstration of inertia. Have students place a marble in a glass. Push the glass along a table in the direction of the opening of the glass. Stop it suddenly. Ask the class: What happened to the marble? Why does it keep moving? Lead the class to the definition of inertia.

• Have students discuss some of their experiences with the forces of inertia, for example:

   Driving in a car when it suddenly stops.
   Ice skating or roller skating and means of stopping.

• Explain to the class that once we get an object in motion, it will tend to stay in motion unless acted upon by another force. In space science, there are two forces working in opposition to one another—one is called gravity, the other is centrifugal force. When these two are in balance, a satellite stays in orbit. (NOTE: These two forces are never in perfect balance.)

• Demonstration. Have a student hold a bowl with a marble in it. While he holds the bowl, ask the class: What is happening to the marble? (Gravity is keeping it at rest at the bottom of the bowl.) How can we "launch" the marble? (Swirl the bowl.) What happens to the marble? (It goes into "orbit" along the sides of the bowl.) What happens if the swirling of the bowl is increased? (The marble flies out of the bowl.) What happens if the speed is decreased? (Marble drops to the bottom of the bowl.) Ask volunteers to relate this demonstration to space travel.

• Have each student bring in the following materials and arrange them as shown in Figure 8-3.

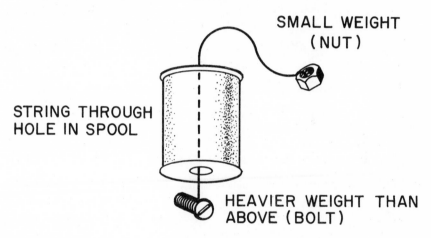

Figure 8-3

• Have each student pretend that the small weight is the payload (satellite), the bottom weight is gravity, the spool is the earth, and their hands and wrists are the rockets.

• Hold spool still. What happens to the payload? (Pulled to earth-spool by gravity.)

• Start twirling the weight by rotating the spool with your hand and wrist. What happens to the payload? (It goes around and swings outward.) What happens to the bottom weight, gravity? (It decreases because it rises to the spool.) Thus, speed is causing the lighter weight to overcome the pull of the heavier weight.

- Increase the speed of the satellite (top weight). What happens? (Pulls heavier weight to bottom of the spool.) Decrease speed of the payload. What happens? (It starts coming back to earth (spool) and bottom weight increases its pull.)
- *Ask:* Can someone tell me how a satellite stays in orbit? (Speed sets up a centrifugal force, *outer push*, which balances or counteracts the force of gravity.)
- Relate this activity to the space flights of several of the astronauts. How did they get into orbit? How was their orbit maintained? How did they change their orbit? How did they reenter the earth's atmosphere? What is meant by *perigee* and *apogee?* Do these words help tell us something about the relationship between gravity and centrifugal force?
- Have each student review the demonstrations, defining in their own words the concepts of inertia, acceleration, gravity, and centrifugal force.

Problem: How does Newton's Third Law of Motion help explain the principles of rocketry?

Generalization: The principle of a rocket engine is based on Newton's Third Law of Motion: For every action there is an equal and opposite reaction. The energy of expanding gases can cause a vehicle to move. The thrust of a rocket propellant is the amount of force it produces.

Content:

- ▶ Introduce Newton's Third Law of Motion.
- ▶ Guide children to state the principle in their own words. This should be a result of the activities and experiments.
- ▶ Reinforce the idea that a rocket engine operates on the action–reaction principle.
- ▶ Bring out the fact that the thrust of a rocket propellant is the thrust of force it produces.
- ▶ Introduce the Saturn V rocket engine.

Informational Activities

- Develop idea of action–reaction with children. Have student put on roller skates and throw an object. In which direction does student move, and why?
- Measuring. Have student on skates. Use a one lb. object. Mark spot where student is standing. Have student throw the object and mark the spot where it lands. Measure how far the student has moved. Use a two lb. object. A three lb. object. Determine if weight of the object makes a difference.
- Construct a chart to determine if there is a correlation between the distance which the object travels and the distance that the student moves.
- From this data, have students predict the distance a skater will move when the object is thrown a specific distance.
- Release an inflated balloon. Discuss why it behaves as it does.
- Using a balance scale, measure thrust by allowing the air from a balloon to hit against the balance pan.
- Experiment and then discuss how the amount of energy in the balloon can be increased.
- Ask students to collect pictures showing action–reaction. Develop a bulletin board display.

    Examples:
    Lawn sprinklers, firearms, cannons, boy stepping from a boat, person holding a hose, etc.

- Observe and feel thrust by using a hose. Discuss why the hose moves. In what direction does it move? What happens when water pressure is increased? Decreased?
- Divide the class into groups and have them design and construct action–reaction engines using milk cartons, wire, rubber bands, balloons, roller skates. If they need ideas, there are many books available showing the different types of engines. Encourage the groups to modify and improve on designs that are found in books. Have each group demonstrate and explain their project to the rest of the class.

- Discuss the Saturn V engine. Develop the following: The weight of the Apollo is 3000 tons. The rocket thrust must be greater than this. Different stages will produce different amounts of thrust. The job of the combined stages is to accelerate a 45 ton payload to a speed of 25,000 mph.
- Have pupils research the Saturn V engine and relate their findings to the principles learned in this unit. Arouse interest and curiosity in Project Apollo, our nation's current venture towards putting a man on the moon.

> NASA publications—Write to National Aeronautics and Space Administration, Washington, D.C. 20546, Publications Branch AFEE-1

Culminating the Unit—Summarizing Activities

■ Have students develop skits depicting the scientific principle involved in lift-off, orbiting, and reentry. "Act out" other principles and have youngsters attempt to determine what is being shown. Examples: inertia, force, balance, gravity, weightlessness, etc.

■ Prepare a school science display around the theme: The History of Space Flight.

■ Have students prepare demonstrations using the principles learned in this unit. Present them to youngsters in other classrooms.

■ Invite a scientist, science writer, or high school science teacher to talk to the class about space flight. Have students prepare questions in advance of the talk.

■ Have class, a committee, or interested individuals read myths and legends concerning the universe and outer space and discuss them in terms of present day knowledge.

■ Read and report about such men as;

Robert Goddard	Wernher von Braun
Hermann Oberth	Konstantin Ziolkovsky

■ If possible, have the class view an actual space shot on television.

Evaluation Techniques

Observation of Youngsters

1. During discussion—
   (*a*) Interest   (*b*) Contributions

2. During experiments—
   (*a*) Use of materials   (*b*) Participation
                 (*c*) Making inferences

3. During group work—
   (*a*) Works effectively with others
   (*b*) Makes a contribution to the group's efforts

4. During individual projects—
   (*a*) Interest   (*b*) Initiative

Written Test on Information Gained in the Unit

DIRECTIONS: Underline the correct answer.

1. The earth is a
   (*a*) meteor   (*c*) star
   (*b*) *planet*   (*d*) sun

2. A scale can be used as an example of
   (*a*) inertia   (*c*) distance
   (*b*) stage   (*d*) *gravity*

3. The base or area from which most of our rockets are launched is
   (*a*) Cape Johnson   (*c*) Cape Hope
   (*b*) Cape Horn   (*d*) *Cape Kennedy*

4. A method using three stages of a rocket to get it into space is described as the
   (*a*) stage principle   (*c*) *step principle*
   (*b*) booster principle   (*d*) counting principle

5. The moon revolving around the earth is an example of a
   (*a*) payload   (*c*) stage
   (*b*) planet   (*d*) *satellite*

6. The earth might be described as a satellite of the
   (*a*) universe   (*c*) *sun*
   (*b*) moon   (*d*) star

7. For a satellite to stay in orbit what two forces must almost balance each other
(*a*) gravity and centripetal force
(*b*) *gravity and centrifugal force*
(*c*) gravity and inertia
(*d*) gravity and satellites

8. If you take a marble, put it in a cup, push the cup and then stop it suddenly, the marble will keep going. This experiment demonstrates the principle of
(*a*) friction   (*c*) speed
(*b*) gravity   (*d*) *inertia*

9. The section of a rocket or spacecraft that gives it that extra push at takeoff is called a
(*a*) blast-off   (*c*) nose cone
(*b*) *booster*   (*d*) pad

10. The force which tends to draw all things away from the center of the earth is
(*a*) *centrifugal force*   (*c*) magnetism
(*b*) centripetal force   (*d*) gravity

11. The tendency of an object to remain at rest or if moving to remain in motion is called
(*a*) *inertia*   (*c*) acceleration
(*b*) resistance   (*d*) force

12. The largest of these planets is
(*a*) Neptune   (*c*) Mars
(*b*) Mercury   (*d*) *Jupiter*

13. The earth revolves around the sun once every
(*a*) 300 days   (*c*) month
(*b*) *365 days*   (*d*) decade

14. Russia sent up bigger rockets and space vehicles because their rockets had greater
(*a*) *thrust*   (*c*) chambers
(*b*) scientists   (*d*) propellers

15. Distance in space is measured in
(*a*) centuries   (*c*) space years
(*b*) *light years*   (*d*) thousand years

16. A force acting upon an object causes it to move in the direction of the
    (*a*) planets   (*c*) earth
    (*b*) North pole   (*d*) *force*

17. When you light a match you have to rub it against a rough surface. When you do this you make use of
    (*a*) inertia   (*c*) *friction*
    (*b*) momentum   (*d*) gravity

18. The rate of increase in the speed of an object is called
    (*a*) motion   (*c*) power
    (*b*) *acceleration*   (*d*) momentum

19. If you wanted to explain the principle of rocketry you could best use a
    (*a*) ball   (*c*) *balloon*
    (*b*) bat   (*d*) top

20. The word that means the space between planets or within the region of planets is
    (*a*) interstellar   (*c*) *interplanetary*
    (*b*) galaxy   (*d*) universal

21. A word used to describe the problem of getting a space man back to earth is
    (*a*) *reentry*   (*c*) recall
    (*b*) burning   (*d*) friction

22. The point at which a satellite is closest to the earth is called
    (*a*) *perigee*   (*c*) apogee
    (*b*) pedigree   (*d*) umbra

23. The path or orbit of satellites takes the form of an
    (*a*) *ellipse*   (*c*) circle
    (*b*) eclipse   (*d*) square

24. Apogee is the point at which a satellite's position from the earth is
    (*a*) *farthest*   (*c*) closest
    (*b*) tracked   (*d*) on radar

25. Rockets are used for space travel because they can fly without
    (*a*) gas   (*c*) motors
    (*b*) wings   (*d*) *air*

26. The U. S. Government Space Agency has the initials
    (*a*) *NASA*   (*c*) USSA
    (*b*) NSTA   (*d*) AASA

27. An increase in motion of an object by force is called
    (*a*) steering   (*c*) boosters
    (*b*) *acceleration*   (*d*) ellipse

28. The force of gravity, as you go away from the earth
    (*a*) increases   (*c*) stays the same
    (*b*) *decreases*   (*d*) accelerates

29. A rocket used for military (war) purposes is called a
    (*a*) bomb   (*c*) spy
    (*b*) *missile*   (*d*) booster

30. The earth moves around the sun in an
    (*a*) axis   (*c*) hour
    (*b*) eclipse   (*d*) *orbit*

31. The center of the solar system is
    (*a*) Earth   (*c*) Mars
    (*b*) *sun*   (*d*) North Star

32. An artificial satellite might be thought of as
    (*a*) a planet   (*c*) a meteor
    (*b*) a Russian country (*d*) *a man-made moon*

33. When a car in which you are riding stops quickly you are thrown forward because of the law of
    (*a*) *inertia*   (*c*) falling bodies
    (*b*) gravity   (*d*) speed

34. To get into space man must use
    (*a*) jets   (*c*) *rockets*
    (*b*) planes   (*d*) wings

35. The push given to a rocket by its engines is called
    (*a*) *thrust*   (*c*) g-force
    (*b*) blast-off   (*d*) burnout

36. The earth goes around the sun once every
    (*a*) five months   (*c*) sixteen months
    (*b*) *twelve months*   (*d*) month

37. A force which seems to draw all things to the earth is
    (*a*) *gravity*   (*c*) inertia
    (*b*) centrifugal force   (*d*) centripetal force

38. The planets go around the
    (*a*) earth   (*c*) *sun*
    (*b*) moon   (*d*) universe

39. A main problem of man's travels is his coming back to
    the earth through the
    (*a*) meteorites   (*c*) cosmic rays
    (*b*) *atmosphere*   (*d*) gravity

40. The path of a satellite is best described as its
    (*a*) orbit   (*c*) *ellipse*
    (*b*) circle   (*d*) eclipse

41. As we go higher in space the air pressure
    (*a*) stays the same   (*c*) *decreases*
    (*b*) increases   (*d*) gets warmer

42. In order to reach space, a rocket needs accurate firings
    of its first, second and third
    (*a*) *stages*   (*c*) jets
    (*b*) flights   (*d*) payload

43. Atomic rays that space scientists believe may be a
    problem in space travel are
    (*a*) ultraviolet rays   (*c*) sun rays
    (*b*) *cosmic rays*   (*d*) opaque rays

44. A "shooting star" is a name given to a falling
    (*a*) *meteor*   (*c*) star
    (*b*) planet   (*d*) rays

45. The science of space flight is called
    (*a*) astronomy   (*c*) *aeronautics*
    (*b*) aerospace   (*d*) astronautics

46. If a meteorite is called a "messenger from space," then
    a "messenger to space" would be called a
    (*a*) electrolyte   (*c*) *satellite*
    (*b*) radiosonde   (*d*) shooting star

47. When a rocket is getting ready for takeoff, it must be placed on
    (*a*) an air base   (*c*) a landing platform
    (*b*) *a launching pad*   (*d*) an aircraft

48. Space is best described as the
    (*a*) *place beyond the atmosphere*
    (*b*) endless universe
    (*c*) beyond the blue sky
    (*d*) relative unknown without air

49. A rocket's speed increases because the rocket
    (*a*) gets a greater push
    (*b*) *becomes lighter because its fuel is used up*
    (*c*) goes into orbit
    (*d*) creates inertia

50. Combustion is another word for
    (*a*) oxygen   (*c*) *burning*
    (*b*) lightning   (*d*) friction

51. Air is necessary for
    (*a*) *combustion*   (*c*) rocket lift-off
    (*b*) propulsion   (*d*) burn-out

52. The stage of a rocket is called the
    (*a*) thrust   (*c*) *booster*
    (*b*) chamber   (*d*) payload

53. The steel and concrete support on which a missile or rocket is placed for takeoff is
    (*a*) an air strip   (*c*) a space building
    (*b*) *a launching pad*   (*d*) a platform

54. A major problem of getting an object into space is the force needed to overcome
    (*a*) *gravity*   (*c*) atmospheric pressure
    (*b*) friction   (*d*) weather

55. The basic principle of rocket motion is best explained by the statement
    (*a*) what goes up must come down
    (*b*) *to every action there is a reaction*
    (*c*) to every pull there is a push
    (*d*) heat causes expansion

56. A space ship coming back to earth would have a problem because the atmosphere would cause it to
   (a) *heat up*   (c) use its fuel
   (b) freeze   (d) lose weight

57. The farther an object goes from the earth, the less is its
   (a) force   (c) *weight*
   (b) orbit   (d) size

58. The point in flight when all fuel is used and the rocket motor stops is called
   (a) breakdown   (c) second stage
   (b) *burnout*   (d) stall-out

59. The force causing an object moving in a circular path to move away from the center of rotation is called
   (a) *centrifugal force*   (c) g-force
   (b) centripetal force   (d) force of friction

60. The force that man will experience when his spaceship takes off is called
   (a) x-force   (c) inertia
   (b) centripetal force   (d) *g-force*

PROJECT APOLLO

Project Mercury and Project Gemini have made significant strides toward putting a man on the moon. It is Project Apollo, however, that will finally make this dream a reality. The success of this project will surely be one of man's most outstanding achievements. This unit will attempt to show the relationship of machines and laws of nature to the Apollo and its crew.

Objectives

1. To develop an understanding of scientific principles related to space travel.
2. To develop an understanding of how man must work with the laws of nature to accomplish scientific goals.
3. To develop skills in scientific investigation and procedures.

  4. To develop an interest in science and other space related
       activities.
  5. To appreciate the contributions that the space program
       has made to everyday living.

Initiating the Unit—Motivational Activities

■ Arrange a bulletin board showing a group of astronauts in a
rocket aimed at the moon.
■ Provide a variety of books and magazines that deal with
space, rockets, gravity, and astronauts.
■ Have mock-ups of rockets if they are available.
■ Show the film:

> *Exploring the Moon*—16 minutes
> McGraw-Hill Text-Films

■ Follow-up discussion should include the way man will most
likely arrive on the moon, aboard an Apollo spacecraft.
■ Show the film:

> *Project Apollo—Manned Flight to the Moon*—13 minutes
> National Aeronautics and Space Administration Film

■ As this film also brings in the Gemini spacecraft, it would be
desirable at this point to briefly cover the background and highlights of the Mercury and Gemini programs. An understanding
of these programs is necessary to appreciate the significance of
Project Apollo.
■ (Check with your nearest film rental library to secure these
and other films and filmstrips mentioned.)

Developing the Unit—Informational Activities

Problem: How can we prove that gravity and inertia acting
on the Apollo capsule will produce an orbit?

Generalization: Our weight shows how much gravity pulls
on us. For every action there is an equal and opposite reaction.

Content:

▶ Develop these principles:
  An object at rest tends to remain at rest.

An object in motion remains in motion unless an outside force is applied.

Motion is in line with the applied force.

Informational Activities

• Demonstrations.

> *Object at rest—*
>
> Place an object on a marked square and develop the idea that it will not move unless a force is applied.
>
> Now place the object on a piece of paper and develop the idea that the object moved when the paper was pulled because of a force (friction).
>
> *Object in motion—*
>
> Place a doll in a box. Push the box forward rapidly. When the box suddenly comes to rest, the doll will continue to travel in a forward motion.
>
> *Motion in line with force—*
>
> Rotate a drill with a wooden circle attached. Have a student sprinkle water on the disk as it is being rotated. In what direction does the water spin off the disk?

As a result of these demonstrations, have the students state Newton's First Law of Motion in their own words.

• Problem-solving.

Divide youngsters into groups. Give each group the following equipment with which to solve the problem of getting an object into orbit around the earth:

> String
>
> Marking pen
>
> Variety of objects to represent rocket
>
> Plywood board with dowel in center, dowel representing the earth
>
> Rubber bands

Have each group appoint a chief engineer whose job it will be to insure that the scientific method of thinking is used. Appoint someone to record the activities of the group in a log or a diary. At the end of the period, have each group present their findings. Compare findings with other groups to see which one has come up with a workable solution.

Problem: What factors are important in producing an orbit for the Apollo module?

Generalization: Gravity and inertia acting upon the Apollo capsule will produce an orbit.
A high degree of precision is required in aiming Apollo at the moon.

Content:

► Introduce the idea of orbits. What is meant by *suborbital? Orbital?*
► Develop Isaac Newton's principles of orbital flight.
► Discuss possible flight paths that Apollo could use.

Informational Activities

• Newton's principle of orbital flight.
  Have a student gently roll a ball off a table and mark the spot where it falls. Repeat several times, using more force with each try. Mark the point at which the ball falls and compare distance with force used. What does this tell us?
• Using a different sized ball, try the same experiment. What conclusions can the students develop?
• Discuss possible flight paths of Apollo. Cut circles, ellipses, parabolas, and hyperbolas out of construction paper. Discuss what observations can be made about the shapes.
• Work out orbits of previous space flights.
  Prepare charts.

Problem: What are the greatest difficulties Apollo will have to overcome?

Generalization: A high degree of precision is required in aiming Apollo at the moon.
Because of the moon's movement, a rocket ship must be aimed ahead of the moon in its orbit. A moving rocket must land on a moving planet.

Content:

▶ Discussion of the difficulties that will be encountered in any attempt to land on the moon.

▶ Discussion of natural laws which must be considered in attempting to land a moving rocket on a moving planet.

Informational Activities

• Draw a large circle on the playground or other suitable area. Have a student representing the earth, stand in the center of the circle. The "moon" starts moving quickly around the "Earth" and the "Earth" rotates in the center of the circle. While they are both in motion, give a "rocket" (ball) to the "Earth" and have "Earth" try to land the "rocket" on the "moon." Have several youngsters try this. Discuss difficulties involved and attempt to solve this problem.

• Develop a chart showing how far Apollo would miss the moon if its flight path was one degree in error.

• Show filmstrips:

> *Rocket Power for Space Travel*—Jam Handy Organization
> *What Are Satellites?*—Jam Handy Organization

Problem: What are some of the problems of survival man faces in space?

Generalization: The farther away something is from the center of the earth, the weaker is the pull of gravity. Weightlessness occurs when the pull of gravity is counterbalanced by inertia. To survive in space, man must wear a pressurized space suit or remain in a pressurized capsule. G-forces are those forces that act upon a man's body as he is being accelerated.

Content:

▶ Discuss what is meant by *weightlessness.*

▶ Discuss the effects of high and low pressure on the human body.

► Develop an understanding of g-forces and their effect on the astronauts.

Informational Activities

• Continue to develop the "space dictionary" by adding new words as they come up.
• Show film:

> *First Men into Space*—16 minutes
> Encyclopaedia Britannica Films, Inc.

• Conduct experiments such as the following to show the effects of air pressure,

1. Pour ½ cup of water into a one gallon can and heat water until it boils. Cap can tightly and remove it from the heat. Observe what happens as it cools. Discuss.
2. Have youngsters search out other experiments related to air pressure. Have them prepare and present them to the class. Discuss in terms of their significance to the effects on the human body.

• Problem-solving.
How can we show or demonstrate weightlessness? Is it possible to have a state of weightlessness on earth? How are astronauts given the experience of a state of weightlessness?
• Show filmstrips:

> *Man in Space*—Society for Visual Education
> *Hazards in Space Travel*—Eyegate House

• We can observe g-forces by placing a small doll in a transparent container with a screw type lid. Punch two holes in the lid and pull through a heavy cord. Screw the lid on tightly and swing it around. The doll will be forced to the bottom. Why?

Problem: What are the most recent developments in the Apollo program?

Generalization: Man is constantly developing new ways to explore and conquer the mysteries of space.

Content:

► Apollo will attempt to send live pictures from space via television to American home viewers.
► Television coverage of the first landing on the moon is also planned.
► Other content in this area will be supplied by keeping up on current happenings.

Informational Activities

• Have youngsters bring in newspaper articles, magazine articles and pictures and put together a class scrapbook.
• Select a committee to write to:

  1. National Aerospace Educational Council
     Dept. B 63
     1025 Connecticut Ave. N.W.
     Washington, D.C.
  2. Superintendent of Documents
     United States Government Printing Office
     Washington, D.C.
  3. U.S. Department of Health, Education and Welfare
     Office of Education
     Washington, D.C.

• Find out what publications these sources have available.

Problem: What contributions has the space program made to other areas of American life?

Generalization: Our space program has made many contributions to everyday life. Our space program benefits all Americans, and in some ways benefits people of other nations.

Content:

► Discuss how the space program has made significant contributions in the areas of:

  1. Industry—new products
  2. Communications
  3. Weather prediction and control

4. International cooperation
5. Add others to list

Informational Activities

• Have youngsters investigate what products have resulted from our space effort. Which of these products are in current use?
• Have a committee report on recent developments in communications related to satellites.
• Have a committee investigate implications for weather study.
• Cite instances showing international cooperation in space related activities.
• Add other investigations as they are introduced by the class.

Culminating the Unit—Summarizing Activities

■ Develop a time line starting with the launching of the first man-made satellite.

■ Have a "panel of experts" prepare a television program where they inform the "public" about Project Apollo.

■ Have children construct models of Apollo and other rockets. Give demonstrations using the principles acquired in the unit concerning lift-off, orbiting, and reentry.

■ Have students prepare a filmstrip for presentation on the opaque projector simulating the actual launching of Apollo. Make use of the principles of rocketry learned in the unit.

■ Have students act out what an astronaut would experience during lift-off, reentry, etc.

Evaluation Techniques

Observation of Youngsters

1. During discussion—
   (*a*) Interest   (*b*) Contributions
2. During experiments—
   (*a*) Use of materials   (*b*) Participation
                (*c*) Making inferences
3. During group work—
   (*a*) Works effectively with others
   (*b*) Makes a contribution to the group's efforts
4. During individual projects—
   (*a*) Interest   (*b*) Initiative

Written Test on Information Gained in the Unit

DIRECTIONS: Underline the correct answer.

1. For a satellite to stay in orbit what two forces must almost balance each other?
    (a) gravity and centripetal force
    (b) *gravity and centrifugal force*
    (c) gravity and inertia
    (d) gravity and satellites

2. If you take a marble, put it in a cup, push the cup and then stop it suddenly, the marble will keep going. This experiment demonstrates the principle of
    (a) friction   (c) speed
    (b) gravity   (d) *inertia*

3. The procedure for checking each system before a rocket launching using inverse numerical order is called a
    (a) mock-up   (c) checkup
    (b) *countdown*   (d) takeoff

4. The force which tends to draw all things away from the center of the earth is
    (a) *centrifugal force*   (c) magnetism
    (b) centripetal force   (d) gravity

5. The tendency of an object to remain at rest or if moving to remain in motion is called
    (a) *inertia*   (c) acceleration
    (b) resistance   (d) force

6. The rate of increase in the speed of an object is called
    (a) motion   (c) power
    (b) *acceleration*   (d) momentum

7. The path or orbit of satellites takes the form of
    (a) *an ellipse*   (c) a circle
    (b) an eclipse   (d) a square

8. An increase in moton of an object by force is called
    (a) steering   (c) boosters
    (b) *acceleration*   (d) ellipse

9. The force of gravity, as you go away from the earth
    (a) increases   (c) stays the same
    (b) *decreases*   (d) accelerates

10. When a car in which you are riding stops quickly you
    are thrown forward because of the law of
    (*a*) *inertia*   (*c*) falling bodies
    (*b*) gravity   (*d*) speed

11. The push given to a rocket by its engine is called
    (*a*) *thrust*   (*c*) g-force
    (*b*) blast-off   (*d*) burnout

12. A force which seems to draw all things to the earth is
    (*a*) *gravity*   (*c*) inertia
    (*b*) centrifugal force   (*d*) centripetal force

13. The feeling of not knowing what is up or down, or
    being at zero gravity is called
    (*a*) gravity   (*c*) inertia
    (*b*) *weightlessness*   (*d*) aerospace

14. The force causing an object moving in a circular path
    to move away from the center of rotation is called
    (*a*) *centrifugal force*   (*c*) g-force
    (*b*) centripetal force   (*d*) force of friction

15. The force that man will experience when his spaceship
    takes off is called
    (*a*) x-force   (*c*) inertia
    (*b*) centripetal force   (*d*) *g-force*

DRAW A PICTURE OR DIAGRAM SHOWING THE FOLLOWING
PRINCIPLES:

16. Inertia
17. Friction
18. Centrifugal force
19. Action–reaction
20. Acceleration

THE ASTRONAUTS

No other science topic is quite as exciting to children of all
ages as is space travel. The men who have explored this latest
frontier are our new heroes. They have succeeded in making
Buck Rogers a reality. Teachers and students alike can share

in exploring the universe through the exploits of our astronauts. It is an exciting and fascinating area to bring into the classroom.

This unit will concentrate on the "star sailors," and deal with them as human beings who are carefully trained, both mentally and physically, for their adventure. Space equipment and supplies needed to keep the astronauts alive and safe are also given consideration here. Children will see that there are still many problems to be solved, but that progress towards solution is being made. It is important that youngsters be made aware of man's ingenuity throughout this study, for it is this quality that will no doubt enable man to overcome the many problems which still exist in this newest realm of exploration.

Objectives

1. To develop an understanding of the rigors of space exploration.
2. To develop an awareness of how man adapts to his environment, and in some instances changes his environment.
3. To develop an appreciation of man's attempt to solve and conquer the universe.

Initiating the Unit—Motivational Activities

■ Arrange a bulletin board with pictures of Mercury and Gemini astronauts. Use newspapers, magazines and NASA publications to obtain pictures.

■ Have children prepare questions that they would like answered in the course of the unit. *Examples:*

Can a man eat in a weightless state?
What would happen to an astronaut if his pressurized suit failed?
How can I become an astronaut?

■ Prepare a book display dealing with men in the space program.

■ Start a collection of articles concerning the astronauts. Use both back issues and current issues of newspapers and magazines. Make a class "magazine" with these articles.

■ Show the film:

> *The John Glenn Story*—Available on free loan, through
> NASA, from the film library in your area. Write to the Na-
> tional Aerospace Education Council for more information.

Developing the Unit—Informational Activities

Problem: Who are the astronauts?

Generalization: The astronauts are a carefully selected group
of men. An increasing number of men comprise the group
of astronauts. Each astronaut has a life and family similar
to our own.

Content:

► Emphasize:

1. The astronauts are carefully selected.
2. They are highly trained for their work.
3. They are "specialists."

► Present data on each of the astronauts.
► Stress the idea of "normal individual" with extraordinary
  qualities and a high degree of training.

Informational Activities

• Have children do research to find the names of the astronauts
  who have made a flight.
• Form committees and have each committee develop a biographical sketch of one of the astronauts.

> Booklet—*America's Space Pilots*
> National Aerospace Education Council
> Dept. B 63
> 1025 Connecticut Ave. N.W.
> Washington, D.C.—the cost is 25 cents.

• Have the chairman of each of the above committees act the
  part of the particular astronaut under study. Have the rest of
  the committee act the part of newsmen. Present a news "interview" to the rest of the class.

Problem: How are they selected?

Generalization: The National Aeronautics and Space Administration selects the astronauts. Relatively few men have been selected to date. No women have been selected for the training program.

Content:

► Stress:

1. Astronaut trainees must meet very high standards.
2. All of the men are *volunteers.*
3. Early astronauts were all from some branch of the service, however, civilians (test pilots, scientists, etc.) are also being trained at present.

► Discuss reasons why the United States might be selecting only men for training at this time.
► Present the role of women in our space program. Explore contributions, employment possibilities, etc.

Informational Activities

• Have children list the qualities they think an astronaut must have. Have them give reasons why these qualities would be important.
• Have children conduct interviews of "potential astronauts." What kinds of qualifications would be required? What kinds of questions would they ask in an interview?
• Panel discussion or debate.
  Is there a place for women in the space program? (Include potential in space-related fields.)

Problem: What are their qualifications?

Generalization: Astronauts are professionals who are highly skilled.
They are in top condition, both mentally and physically.

Content:

▶ List necessary qualifications such as mental and physical health, test pilot training, engineering graduate, ability to think and react quickly, endurance, etc.

▶ Discuss mental and physical health. Relate this to the habits the children should seek to acquire.

Informational Activities

• Develop a chart or devote a section of a bulletin board to Good Mental Health. Include cheerfulness, optimism, interest, friendliness, etc.

• Develop a chart or devote a section of a bulletin board to Good Health Habits. Include cleanliness, exercise, balanced meals, plenty of sleep, appropriate clothing, etc.

• Have youngsters plan balanced meals for the astronauts.

• Have the class write paragraphs using character traits as subjects.

Problem: What special training is involved?

Generalization: Astronauts receive intensive training in *all* phases of the space flight program. Their lives depend on their training.

Content:

▶ Emphasize:

1. After an astronaut has been accepted, he is assigned to a particular phase of the space flight as a project engineer.

2. Each astronaut knows the action of *every* piece of equipment on board.

3. Besides being trained in engineering and flight, they have much knowledge in related fields such as natural science, astronomy, anatomy, physiology, astrogation, etc.

▶ Present a sketch of the training that the astronauts undergo in flight trainers, simulators, and centrifuges.

Informational Activities

* Prepare an Astronaut's Handbook of Terms and have young-sters use this means to expand and enrich their vocabulary.
* Have the class work out demonstrations employing some of the scientific principles used in training. Show the filmstrips:

    Travel in Space and *Man in Space*—Encyclopaedia Britan-nica Films, Inc.
    Man Travels in Space—Eyegate House
    Getting Ready for a Space Trip—Jam Handy Organization

* Demonstrations:
    1. Weightlessness. Discuss the possibilities and problems of showing weightlessness. One demonstration which comes close is by using a glass jar partially filled with water and a cork. Drill a small hole in the lid of the jar. Fasten a cork to a piece of coathanger wire and slip it through the lid, so that the cork can be held at the bottom of the jar. If the wire is released the cork will come to the surface. If the jar is dropped from the top of a ladder, however, the cork will not rise until the jar ceases to fall. Let the jar drop onto a blanket held securely at the corners.

* Filmstrip:

    Man in Space—Society for Visual Education

    2. Acceleration and Deceleration. Put a doll in a box and place the box on a roller skate. Pull the skate quickly across the room. Observe what happens when doll has her back against the front of the box. Repeat the experi-ment, observing above action if the box is suddenly slowed down.
    3. Heat Stress. Using a light bulb to represent the sun, show the effects of intense heat on an object. Place the object near the "sun" and observe the differences in tempera-ture between the side nearest sun and the opposite side.
    4. Add others and encourage the children to develop suit-able experiments.

- Have students who are interested in astronomy:
    1. Make a telescope.
    2. Make charts of the heavens.
    3. Give reports on celestial navigation.
    4. Do research on various observatories and relate their findings to our space program.
    5. Give reports on famous persons such as Galileo and Maria Mitchell.

- Show filmstrips:

    Astronomy Through the Ages—
    Man Becomes an Astronomer—
    The Stars—
    Encyclopaedia Britannica Films, Incorporated

Problem: What is needed to survive in space?

Generalization: In order to survive in space, man must be provided with an environment similar to that of Earth.

Content:

- ► Discuss the elements that are needed for survival such as special clothing, special food, special equipment, etc.
- ► Develop the purpose of wearing "space suits." Using their knowledge of space, have youngsters supply reasons for wearing a special garment.
- ► Emphasize:
    1. A full pressure suit is needed in order to keep a man surrounded by five pounds of air pressure per square inch.
    2. Parts of the suit can be removed if cabin pressure is kept up.
    3. The space suit protects the astronaut from either extreme of temperature.
    4. Equipment attached to the suit supplies oxygen for breathing.
    5. The suit is made of very sturdy material to keep meteoroids, etc. from penetrating.

6. The suit is designed to protect the men from radiation hazard.
7. Other equipment is a part of the suit, all designed for the astronaut's needs and safety.

► Discuss the problems of food in a space capsule. Does weightlessness have any influence on the types of foods used?
► Emphasize:
1. New methods of food preparation and storage have been developed.
2. Many of these innovations have entered our daily lives.
3. Food has a psychological as well as a physical effect on a man.
4. Astronauts may have to "grow" some of their food for long distance flights.

► Develop the idea that much special equipment is needed by the astronauts in order to survive in space.

Informational Activities

• Have a brainstorming session and list possible dangers in space for an "earth man."
• Collect pictures of space suits. Compare earlier Mercury suits with Gemini and Apollo suits.
• Show filmstrip:

  Getting Ready for a Space Trip—
  Jam Handy Organization

• Art project. Have youngsters design space suits and give reasons for changes they have made.
• Show filmstrip:

  How an Astronaut Lives in Space—
  Filmstrip House

• Discuss weightlessness and its effect on eating and drinking. Can you drink water in a weightless state? Is it necessary to have special containers? Can you swallow without gravity? Have a child drink water while standing upside down.

- Filmstrip:

  Hazards in Space Travel—Eyegate House

- Using a calorie chart, have youngsters determine how many calories a man needs a day. Develop a well balanced menu based on these figures.
- Extend the above activity by

  1. Making a list of all foods one man will need for a 14-day trip, at three meals a day.
  2. Since Apollo is a three man mission, how much food will be necessary?
  3. Apollo hopes to travel to the moon. How long will this take? How much food is required for this flight?
  4. A trip to Mars may take two and a half years. This means approximately *five tons* of food per man. How would the class solve the problem that this poses?

- Discuss the psychological effect of food. Pose this problem— Could man survive on nutrient packed capsules? Have children write a paragraph supporting their position.
- Have youngsters design new packaging for food used in space. (Containers you could eat, etc.) Devise new methods of preparing food.
- Have the class make a list of foods and/or processes which have made their way to our grocers' shelves because of space research, such as freeze-drying, etc.
- Have the class check newspaper accounts of space missions and report on what foods were taken along.
- Divide the class into committees. Have each committee research one area of special equipment.

  1. Communications equipment   4. Electronic devices
  2. Medical equipment   5. Ejection equipment
  3. Tools   6. Molded seats, etc.

- Have the class make charts showing this special equipment. Label and describe the function of each item.

Problem: What problems still remain?

Generalization: There are still many problems to be solved in space flight. The lunar mission presents problems not yet encountered by any astronaut.

Content:

► Study the Van Allen radiation belt and its potential dangers.
► Discuss dangers such as

1. Cosmic rays
2. Meteors
3. Meteor streams

4. Ultraviolet rays
5. Solar flares
6. Temperature extremes

7. Fire

► Discuss problems still remaining with pressure suits, food and water, etc., especially in terms of a lunar mission.

Informational Activities

• Map out the solar system. Draw in the area of the Van Allen radiation belt.
• Interested youngsters may want to give individual reports on such topics as solar flares, meteors, etc.
• Show film:

> *Asteroids, Comets, and Meteorites*—Film Associates of California—11 min.

• Show filmstrip:

> *Comets and Meteors*—Society for Visual Education

Culminating the Unit—Summarizing Activities

■ Have youngsters develop a time line using the astronauts and cosmonauts. Start with Yuri A. Gagarin. Include such items as the date of the launch, name of the astronaut or cosmonaut, name of the spacecraft, etc.

■ Have a group of students develop a chart showing the number of orbits each astronaut or team of astronauts completed. Indicate the time in flight.

■ Have the class:
1. Compute the flight distance of the astronauts.
2. Figure out the amount of time (in months and days) elapsing between space shots.
3. Develop math problems using the mileage figures of the various flights.

■ Investigate space careers; astronauts, plus related personnel such as astronomers, engineers, space medics, etc.

■ Have youngsters imagine they are astronauts on a lunar mission. What do they find?
1. Write stories and draw pictures of the lunar surface, possible vegetation, etc.
2. Write letters back to Earth.
3. Tape record messages to be sent back to Earth.
4. Keep a "log" similar to that of a ship captain.

■ Encourage youngsters to write a personal or a class letter to a *real* astronaut.

■ Have groups of youngsters present skits of astronaut teams preparing for a flight, while in flight, and upon landing. Stress use of the concepts and understandings gained from the unit.

Evaluation Techniques

Observation of Youngsters
1. During discussion—
   (a) Interest   (b) Contributions
2. During experiments—
   (a) Use of materials   (b) Participation
                (c) Making inferences
3. During group work—
   (a) Works effectively with others
   (b) Makes a contribution to the group's efforts
4. During individual projects—
   (a) Interest   (b) Initiative

Written Test on Information Gained in the Unit

DIRECTIONS: Underline the correct answer.

1. Radiation particularly dangerous in space travel is
   (*a*) *cosmic rays*   (*c*) alpha rays
   (*b*) ultraviolet rays   (*d*) delta rays

2. The object that man is in when he is sent into space is a
   (*a*) cage   (*c*) boattail
   (*b*) compartment   (*d*) *capsule*

3. Spacemen will have to solve the problem of
   (*a*) cloud chambers   (*c*) comets
   (*b*) *cosmic rays*   (*d*) short stars

4. One of the most difficult problems facing a man living in space will be
   (*a*) food   (*c*) heat
   (*b*) *boredom*   (*d*) planets

5. A spaceship painted black would
   (*a*) *absorb heat*   (*c*) reflect heat
   (*b*) combust   (*d*) humidify

6. A word used to describe the problem of getting a space-man back to Earth is
   (*a*) *reentry*   (*c*) recall
   (*b*) burning   (*d*) friction

7. Of the following types of food, the one that may be used by men in space is
   (*a*) wheat   (*c*) yeast
   (*b*) molds   (*d*) *algae*

8. The first American to orbit the earth was
   (*a*) *John Glenn*   (*c*) Alan Shepard
   (*b*) Virgil Grissom   (*d*) Leroy Cooper

9. A main problem of man's travels is his coming back to the earth through the
   (*a*) meteorites   (*c*) cosmic rays
   (*b*) *atmosphere*   (*d*) gravity

10. Of the following, the name that best describes a space traveler is
    (*a*) scientist   (*c*) engineer
    (*b*) *astronaut*   (*d*) voyager

11. A man in space will weigh
    (a) *less*   (c) the same
    (b) more   (d) twenty pounds

12. The heat and friction that causes an astronaut's problems when coming back to earth is a result of the earth's
    (a) *atmosphere*   (c) rotation
    (b) gravity   (d) oceans

13. If a man is in outer space without a space suit, the lack of air pressure would cause him to
    (a) faint   (c) float
    (b) *explode*   (d) melt

14. A man living in a spaceship can best be compared to a
    (a) *fish in an aquarium*   (c) cat in a dark room
    (b) dog in a doghouse   (d) monkey in the attic

15. A place in which a group of people can live while orbiting the earth is called a
    (a) capsule   (c) *space station*
    (b) space capsule   (d) space pad

SPACE EXPLORATION

References for Children

Astronauts

1. Bergaust, Eriste. *First Men in Space*. New York: G. P. Putnam's Sons, 1960.
2. Branley, Franklin. *A Book of Astronauts for You*. New York: Thomas Y. Crowell Co., 1963.
3. Foley, Scott. *Man in Orbit*. New York: Parent's Magazine, 1962.
4. Hyde, Margaret. *Off into Space*. New York: McGraw-Hill Book Co. Inc., 1959.
5. Kay, Terrence. *Space Volunteers*. New York: Harper and Brothers, 1960.
6. Ley, Willy. *Space Pilots*. New York: The Macmillan Co., 1959.
7. Olney, Ross. *Americans in Space*. Camden, New Jersey: Nelson Press, 1966.
8. Schraff, Robert. *Into Space with the Astronauts*. New York: Grosset and Dunlap, 1965.
9. Shelton, W. R. *Flights of the Astronauts*. Boston: Little, Brown and Co., 1963.

10. Wells, Robert. *What Does an Astronaut Do?* Boston: Little, Brown and Co., 1961.
11. Wells, Robert. *Alive in Space.* Boston: Little, Brown and Co., 1961.

Project Apollo

1. Caidin, Martin. *By Apollo to the Moon.* New York: Julian Messner, Inc., 1963.
2. Chester, Michael and McClinton, David. *The Moon: Target for Apollo.* New York: C. P. Putnam's Sons, 1963.
3. Hill, Robert. *What Moon Astronauts Will Do All Day.* New York: John Day Co., 1963.

Space Exploration

1. Bendick, Jeanne. *First Book of Space Travel.* New York: Franklin Watts, Inc., 1953.
2. Bergaust, Eriste. *Illustrated Space Encyclopedia.* New York: G. P. Putnam's Sons, 1965.
3. Bergaust, Eriste. *Rockets to the Moon.* New York: G. P. Putnam's Sons, 1961.
4. Caidin, Martin. *Why Space? and How It Serves You in Your Daily Life.* New York: Julian Messner, Inc., 1965.
5. Chester, Michael. *Rockets and Space Craft of the World.* New York: W. W. Norton & Company, 1964.
6. Coggins, Jack. *Rockets, Jets, Guided Missiles, and Space Ships.* New York: Random House, 1951.
7. Gottlieb, William. *Space Flight and How It Works.* New York: Doubleday and Co., Inc., 1963.
8. Kane, Elmer. *What Is Space?* Chicago: Benefic Press, 1962.
9. Ley, Willy. *Our Work in Outer Space.* New York: The Macmillan Co., 1964.
10. Lewellen, John. *You and Space Travel.* Chicago: Children's Press, 1958.
11. Nephew, William. *Beyond Mars.* New York: G. P. Putnam's Sons, 1960.
12. Nephew, William. *Planet Trip.* New York: G. P. Putnam's Sons, 1960.
13. Von Braun, Wernher. *First Man to the Moon.* New York: Holt, Rinehart and Winston Co., 1960.

References for Teachers

1. Alexander, Thomas. *Project Apollo: Man to the Moon.* New York: Harper and Row Publishers, 1964.
2. Bell, Joseph. *Seven into Space.* Chicago: Popular Mechanics Co., 1960.
3. Bender, Otto. *Victory in Space.* New York: Walker and Co., 1962.
4. Besserer, C. W. *Guide to the Space Age.* Englewood Cliffs, New Jersey: Prentice-Hall, Inc., 1959.
5. Burgess, Eric. *Satellites and Spaceflight.* New York: The Macmillan Co., 1957.
6. Caidin, Martin. *Rendezvous in Space.* New York: E. P. Dutton Co., Inc., 1962.
7. Caidin, Martin. *Spaceport, U.S.A.* New York: E. P. Dutton Co., Inc., 1959.
8. Clarke, Arthur. *Interplanetary Flight.* New York: Harper and Brothers, 1960.
9. Clarke, Arthur. *The Making of a Moon.* New York: Harper and Brothers, 1957.
10. Cox, Donald. *The Space Race: Sputnik to Apollo . . . and Beyond.* New York: Chilton Co., 1962.
11. DuBridge, Lee. *Introduction to Space.* New York: Columbia University Press, 1960.
12. Haley, Andrew. *Rocketry and Space Exploration.* Princeton: D. Van Nostrand Co., Inc., 1958.
13. Holmes, David. *What Is Going on in Outer Space?* New York: Funk and Wagnalls Co., 1958.
14. Holmes, Jay. *America on the Moon: Enterprise of the Sixties.* Philadelphia: J. P. Lippincott Co., 1962.

Pamphlets

1. *Aerospace* (reprint). F. E. Compton and Co., 1000 N. Dearborn St., Chicago 10, Illinois. Free.
2. *Aeronautics and Space Bibliography.* Superintendent of Documents, U.S. Government Printing Office, Washington, D.C. 30¢.
3. *Earth and Space Guide for Elementary Teachers.* National Aerospace Education Council, Dept. B63, 1025 Connecticut Ave., N.W. Washington 6, D.C. 25¢.

4. *Space—Challenge and Promise.* Aerospace Industries Association, 1725 DeSales St. N.W., Washington 6, D.C. Free.
5. *Space, the New Frontier.* NASA, Educational Publications, AFEE. Washington 25, D.C. Free.
6. *Space Travel* (reprint). Field Enterprises Educational Corporation, Merchandise Mart Plaza, Chicago 54, Illinois. 25¢.
7. *Teaching Children About Space Science.* Communicative Arts, P.O. Box 11017, San Diego 11, California. $1.50.

Films

1. *Gravity: How It Affects Us.* Color or b/w. $150.00 or $75.00. 14 minutes. Encyclopaedia Britannica Films, Inc., Wilmette, Illinois.
2. *Gravity: The Mighty Pull.* Color. $135.00. 13½ minutes. United World Films, Inc., 1445 Park Ave., New York 29, New York.
3. *Mostly Missiles.* b/w. $17.00. Seven minutes. Communicative Arts, P.O. Box 11017, San Diego 11, California.
4. *Rockets and Satellites.* Color. $135.00. 13½ minutes. United World Films, Inc., 1445 Park Ave., New York 29, New York.
5. *Spacemobile.* 1962. Color. 45 minutes. Sound. NASA film. Order from center in your area.
6. *The Big Bounce.* Color. 14 minutes. Free loan. Bell Telephone Co. Apply local office.
7. *The Mastery of Space.* 1962. 58 minutes. Color. Sound. NASA films. Order from center in your area.
8. *The Path to Space.* b/w. 28 minutes. Free loan. Association Films, 347 Madison Ave., New York 17, New York.
9. *What is Space?* Color or b/w. $120.00 or $60.00. 11 minutes. Encyclopaedia Britannica Films, Inc., Wilmette, Illinois.

Filmstrips

1. *Conquering Space.* Color, 49 frames. $14.00, rental $4.50. Includes a 30 minute L.P. reading. Curriculum Materials Corp., 1319 Vine St., Philadelphia 7, Pennsylvania.
2. *Exploring the Space Around Earth.* Color, 63 frames. $7.50. Films for Education, Audio Lane, New Haven, Connecticut.
3. *Hazards in Space Travel.* Color, 36 frames. $4.00. Eyegate House, 146-01 Archer Ave., Jamaica 35, New York.

4. *Man Travels in Space*. Color, 36 frames. $4.00. Eyegate House, 146-01 Archer Ave., Jamaica 35, New York.
5. *Our Solar System*. Color, 29 frames. $5.00. Filmstrip House, 432 Park Avenue South, New York 16, New York.
6. *Space Flight*. Part I, Physical Problems. Color, 41 frames. $6.50. Part II, Human Problems. Color, 41 frames. $6.50. McGraw-Hill Text Films, 330 West 42nd Street, New York 36, New York.
7. *Travel in Space*. Color, 49 frames. $6.00. Encyclopaedia Britannica, Inc., Wilmette, Illinois.
8. *What Are Satellites?* Color, 28 frames. $5.75. Jam Handy Organization, 2821 E. Grand Blvd., Detroit 11, Michigan.

OCEANOGRAPHY

Man's quest for outer space sometimes overshadows many of his other scientific activities. We tend to forget that the Earth is a "water" planet, a planet upon which seventy-five per cent of the surface is occupied by water. The seas and oceans offer man the same challenges as outer space. The ocean harbors many secrets and valuable resources; thus, a study of a relatively young science—oceanography—will prove most meaningful.

The exploration of "inner space" will be as exciting for your students as the adventures of outer space. The problems are similar: exploring, examining, testing the environment; returning to earth with the information; and then planning new investigations. Whether man goes to the heights of space or the depths of oceans, he is faced with, and must solve, many complex problems. This unit holds promise for high motivation, consistent interest, and significant learnings. An expanded subject matter outline is included.

Objectives

1. To develop an understanding of the ocean and its composition.
2. To develop an awareness of how man is constantly attempting to understand and control his environment.
3. To develop an appreciation of our natural environment.

Initiating the Unit—Motivational Activities

■ Have students prepare a bulletin board and start a scrapbook on the ocean. Use newspapers and magazines for articles and pictures.

■ Show the film:

> *The Earth: Its Oceans* 14 minutes
> Coronet films

■ Have students discuss the observable characteristics of the ocean that the film points out, such as the ocean's surface and nonliving and living things in the water. Discuss the importance of oceans to man, and why it will be of great benefit to increase our knowledge of the ocean.

■ Invite a speaker to your class to tell the students what oceanographers do. Have students prepare questions in advance.

■ Invite a person interested in skin diving and scuba diving to display his gear, tell some of the problems of diving, and relate his feelings about being alone in deep water.

■ Have students write letters for information concerning the ocean and oceanographers.

■ Ask students who have been to the ocean to describe their experiences in ocean water. Have them describe the beach, waves and air. If some students have visited both the Atlantic and Pacific oceans, ask them to describe the differences, if any.

Developing the Unit—Informational Activities

Problems: What is oceanography? What do oceanographers do?

Generalization: Oceanography is a relatively new science drawing upon the knowledge of other sciences.
Scientists are investigating the many mysteries of the ocean. There are many "treasures" scientists are trying to discover in the ocean.

Content:

➤ Oceanography (oceanology) is the study of oceans.

➤ Oceanographers are scientists who study the ocean. They specialize in various fields such as geology, chemistry, physics and biology. Thus, there are such sciences as geological oceanography, chemical oceanography, etc.

Informational Activities

• Have students prepare a chart on word derivation in science, starting with

Oceanology—study of the oceans,
Oceanography—mapping or charting the oceans,
Marine biology—study of living things in the water.

• Follow each of these descriptions with the name of the scientist working in this area—example, biologist, zoologist, etc.
• Collect water samples from three sources: an ocean, a lake, and a water tap. Let the water settle for a few days. Examine the bottom of the containers. What do they contain? Why?
• Have students prepare a list of questions they would like answered during the course of this unit. Refer to this list as you develop the concepts in this unit.

Problem: How do oceanographers and navigators find their location in the ocean?

Generalization: Latitude and longitude are systems devised to chart the vast area of the ocean.

Content:

➤ Latitude

1. Think of an imaginary circle around the center of the earth—equator.
2. Circles developed in relation to the equator and going around the earth are called *parallels*.
3. Each parallel has a number. Example, parallel number ten would be latitude ten (North or South).

► Longitude

1. Imaginary lines circling the earth from pole to pole crossing latitude lines.
2. These lines are called *meridians*. They range from 0 to 180 degrees (East or West).

Informational Activities

• Have the students describe the differences between latitude and longitude. To do this they must understand parallel and converging lines. Place a check in the box that describes the concept for latitude and longitude.

	AROUND	PARALLEL	CONVERGING	HORIZONTAL	VER-TICAL	UP & DOWN
LONGITUDE						
LATITUDE						

Figure 8-4

• Use a round, plain rubber ball to show how the early map makers developed the concept of latitude and longitude. Starting at the equator (middle of the ball), draw a line around the ball to represent the equator. Above and below the equator, draw other lines to represent latitudinal lines. For example, this line may represent latitude ten which is about 700 miles above or below the equator. Thus, one represents about 70 miles. These map makers provided a further breakdown of the degree scale, using minutes and seconds. One minute equals about six thousand feet; one second, about one hundred feet.
• Using the same ball, draw lines from one pole to the opposite pole (N–S) and back to the pole where you started. This illustrates lines of longitude. A peeled grapefruit or orange will also illustrate longitudinal lines. The early map makers knew that the Earth rotated 360° every 24 hours. Dividing 360 by 24, they drew meridian (longitudinal) lines every 15°. The prime meridian (0°) passes through the Royal Observa-

tory in Greenwich. The 180th meridian is directly opposite the prime meridian on the other side of the globe.

- Use a globe to discuss both longitude and latitude and to show how one can find a specific place by using these concepts.
- Have students complete the following chart: Figure 8-5.

PLACE	LONGITUDE	LATITUDE
SCHOOL		
N. Y. C.		
WASH. D. C.		
CHICAGO		
LOS ANGELES		
PARIS		
BERLIN		
MOSCOW		

Figure 8-5

- Have students describe the differences between latitude and longitude. To do this, they must know how parallel and converging lines differ. Develop a chart displaying these concepts similar to the one in Figure 8-6.

	PARALLEL	CONVERGING	HORIZONTAL	VERTICAL
LATITUDE				
LONGITUDE				

Figure 8-6

Problem: What are some characteristics of the ocean?

Generalization: A large portion of the surface of the earth is covered by water.
The ocean floor has characteristics similar to land formations.
The ocean is the environment for a variety of plants and animals.
Ocean water is salty.
The ocean contains a wealth of foods and minerals.

Content:

► The ocean

1. covers 75 per cent of the earth's surface.
2. has an area of about 141 million square miles.
3. has an average depth of about 2.35 miles.
4. has a floor area that is mountainous and rugged.
   a) continental shelf
   b) continental slope
   c) mid-ocean mountain range
   d) continental rise
   e) trenches
   f) guyots
5. has a floor of various layers—bottom sediments (top layer), basaltic crust (middle layer), mantel material (lower layer).
6. contains plant and animal life ranging from plankton to whales.
7. is divided into separate life zones because of
   a) pressure
   b) light
   c) temperature
   d) saltiness

Informational Activities

• Encourage the students to cut out and save newspaper and magazine articles on this topic throughout the course of this unit.
• Have the students make a list of all of the major oceans and seas. What is the difference between an ocean and a sea?
• How did oceans and seas get their names? Who named them? Have each student select an ocean or sea and find the answers to these questions. Each student should present an oral report in which he also locates the ocean or sea for the class and answers class questions.
• Have a committee prepare a chart of the ocean floor using a silhouette effect, black on white, and labeling appropriate areas.

- If you live near the ocean, have students collect samples of sand. If you do not live near the ocean, use other beach sand. Students might also write to friends for samples if none are available close by. Use a magnifying glass to examine the grains of sand. Are the grains of different colors? Why? What is sand made of? Are the rocks found near beaches rugged and craggy? Are they smooth? Why?
- To demonstrate that ocean water is salty, place some in a shallow dish. Allow the water to completely evaporate and determine what is left. Tasting will show that salt remains and was contained in the water. If water from the ocean is not available, use ordinary tap water with salt added.

Problem: What are the causes of ocean currents?

Generalization: Ocean currents are caused by the temperature of the water and the prevailing winds.

Content:

► Causes of currents

1. winds
2. water temperature
3. earth's rotation

► Classifications of currents

1. North equatorial current
2. South equatorial current
3. Gulf stream
4. Labrador current

► There are currents in the ocean that are on the surface and there are some under the surface. Some currents move upward, others downward.

► Sargasso Sea

1. area of no current
2. called a floating forest

Informational Activities

- Prepare a large map as a class project. Show the major ocean currents of the world in red and the major air currents in blue.
- Read parts of the book *Kon-tiki* to the class to show how man used currents for sailing and to relate some of the strange experiences the ocean provided for the explorers. (Heyerdahl, T. *Kon-tiki,* Rand McNally & Co., Chicago, 1960)
- To illustrate the effect of temperature on water currents, use a large open mouth glass jar, half full of cold water. In a small test tube, place ink or colored water. Holding your finger over the test tube so that the ink can escape, place the test tube in the jar of water. What happens when you let the ink out of the test tube? Repeat the experiment, this time putting warm water in the jar. What happens now? Will salt affect the results? Repeat the two experiments, but add a cup of salt to the cold and warm water. Do you get different results?

Problem: What causes waves?

Generalization: Waves are the result of winds.

Content:

► Waves

1. are on ocean surface.
2. are caused by winds.
3. are related to the openness of the ocean and the distance the waves travel.
4. are called "swells" if they are long and travel steadily through the water.

Informational Activities

- Have a student fill a bowl with water. Have the class take turns blowing across the rim of the bowl. What happens to the surface water? (ripples) What happens to the water below the surface? (calm) What happens if you blow harder? (larger waves)

- Have students collect pictures and articles on the force of waves. Bascom, "Ocean Waves," *Scientific American.* August 1959. Offprint #828, W. H. Freeman & Co., San Francisco 4, California.
- Swimming in the Atlantic and Pacific oceans can be great fun. Have a student who has had this experience try to describe it, particularly referring to the wave action of these oceans.

Problems: What are ocean tides? What causes them?

Generalization: The ocean reacts to the gravitational attraction of the moon.

Content:

► Tides

1. are defined as the rise and fall of the ocean.
2. are caused by the gravitational attraction of the moon. (Newton's Universal Law of Gravitation)
3. are of two types, high and low.
4. occur every 12 hours or twice a day.
5. result because water moves more easily than land when attracted by the moon's gravitational pull.

Informational Activities

- Show the film:

  Tides—Almanac, 12 minutes

- Have the class explain why clam diggers begin their work when the tide is "out."

- Problems:

  1. If a seven foot pole was inserted in the ocean floor about nine feet from shore, and at high tide the water covered six feet of the pole, would more or less of the pole show at low tide? Why?
  2. When would it be easiest to row a boat to shore—in low or high tide? Why?

Problem: How will the ocean's contents help man's quest for survival?

Generalization: The ocean offers an abundance of untapped resources.

Content:

► Fish Industry
1. oldest industry in the United States
2. great food supply
3. ocean fish supply iodine which is used by the thyroid gland in our body
4. fish oil is used for medicine, soap, linoleum, etc.
5. fish skin is used for belts, billfolds, shoes, etc.

► Scientists are attempting to develop inexpensive methods of changing salt water to fresh usable water.

► Minerals contained in the ocean

1. magnesium
2. phosphate
3. uranium
4. copper
5. manganese
6. bromine
7. sodium chloride
8. gold
9. silver

► Other products
1. Oil—petroleum is obtained by drilling into the ocean floor
2. Kelp—when dried and burned, the ashes help provide certain chemicals
3. Algae—called the "vegetable of the sea" and may be used by man to help feed the world's ever increasing population.

Informational Activities

• Prepare a bulletin board titled Treasures from the Sea. Have students bring in pictures of some of the foods, minerals, and other materials the oceans provide.

Shaw, "The Schooling of Fishes." *Scientific American.* June 1962. Offprint #124, W. H. Freeman & Co., San Francisco 4, California.

- Have students construct a *diorama* illustrating life in the ocean.
- Have students investigate industries resulting from the sea: fishing, whaling, oil drilling, skin diving, sports, treasure-hunting, etc.
- Have students study the symbiotic (living together) life of some sea animals.

    1. Help them understand the difference between a symbiotic relationship and a parasitic relationship.
    2. Give illustrations of this relationshp. *Example,* a whale has barnacles on its hide that ride with him and eat what he leaves. (Lembaugh, "Cleaning Symbiosis," *Scientific American,* August 1961. Offprint #135, W. H. Freeman & Co., San Francisco 4, California.

- Have students collect pictures of fish and other sea animals and plants. Place in the class scrapbook.
- Have small groups of students select a mineral that comes from the sea and find out how man can use it. Develop a class chart after each student has finished his assignment.
- Have students start a collection of seashells. How many different kinds of seashells can they find? Have each student hold a shell to his ear. An old saying claims that "you can hear the ocean." Ask each student what he thinks he hears. If they say "the ocean," ask how this is possible. Explore this problem with the class.
- Show the films:

    We Explore Ocean Life—Coronet, 11 minutes
    Secrets of the Underwater World—Walt Disney Productions, 16 minutes
    Undersea Life—Warner, 20 minutes
    Underwater Adventure—Sterling, 9 minutes

Problem: What are oceanographers planning for the U. S. "Man From the Sea" program?

Generalization: Oceanography has a long history. Men have developed various plans for studying the ocean depths. The problems of sea exploration are similar to the problems of space exploration.

Content:

► Early oceanographers

1. Aristotle
2. Vasco da Gama
3. Magellan
4. James Cook
5. Lt. Matthew Maury—father of American oceanography

► Expeditions

1. 1873–76—Challenger
2. 1925–27—Meteor expedition
3. 1957–58—International Geophysical Year

► Oceanographic Research

1. Lamont Geological Observatory—uses a ship named VEMA
2. Scripps Institute of Oceanography—uses a ship named *Horizon*
3. Woods Hole (Massachusetts) Oceanographic Institution—uses a research vessel named *Atlantic II*
4. Other governmental and educational agencies contribute to oceanographic research

► Man In Sea Programs

1. Bathysphere—Barton and Beebe—August 15, 1934—depth 3028 feet
2. Benthoscope—Barton—1948—depth 4500 feet
3. Bathyscaphe—Piccard—1954—depth 13,284 feet
4. Trieste—Piccard and Walsh—1960—depth 37,800 feet
5. Project Nekton—U.S. Navy—1960—Trieste I and II
6. Sealab I—A forty foot cylinder in which four aquanauts lived for ten days at a depth of 192 feet

7. Sealab II—In this cylindrical capsule, aquanauts lived 205 feet down in the Pacific Ocean for one month.

► Aquanauts

1. Navy Capt. George Bond
2. Cdr. Scott Carpenter (astronaut)
3. Lt. Bob Sonnenberg
4. Others

► Problems of ocean study

1. need for special equipment, food supplies, sea suits, air supply, etc.
2. determining how long man can stand the loneliness and confines of a 40 foot cylindrical sphere.
3. decompression—water pressure
4. exploration of ocean depths by aquanauts leaving the sphere creates problems.

Informational Activities

• Have the class prepare a "history" book on oceanography.

Bailey, "The Voyage of the 'Challenger.' " *Scientific American.* May 1953. Offprint #830. W. H. Freeman & Co., San Francisco 4, California.

• Through the drawings of each student follow the chronology of oceanography as presented in the subject matter outline.
• Divide the class into committees and have each group take a particular phase of the exploration of the ocean as presented in the subject matter outline.
• Have a group of students dramatize the experiments of Sealab II.
• Have teams of students debate the topic: It is better to explore the sea than to explore outer space.
• Experiments with water pressure. Take a large juice can and bore three holes in the can, one hole near the top, one in the center, and one near the bottom. Use tape to cover the holes. Fill the can with water. Remove the tape quickly. Observe what happens. Pressure will cause the water to be forced out

of the holes. Develop a principle from this experiment. (The deeper the water, the greater the water pressure.)

- Discuss the effects of water pressure on underwater experiments, especially as far as the aquanauts are concerned. Relate to the effects of air pressure on the astronauts.
- Show the film:

  Simple Demonstrations With Water—Coronet Films—13 minutes

Problem: What are some devices and equipment man uses to investigate the ocean?

Generalization: Special equipment and supplies are needed for man's ocean exploration.

Content:

► In planning stages
   1. Mesocaph—underwater helicopter
   2. Denise—J. Yves Cousteau designer—two-man diving saucer
   3. Alvin—two-man research submarine
   4. Aluminaut—first aluminum diver

► Special Vessels
   1. FLIP (Floating Instrument Platform)—towed out to sea—tube end is flooded—it then assumes a vertical position.
   2. RUM (Remote Underwater Manipulator)—a television camera that provides scientists with pictures of the ocean floor.
   3. Mr. Mobot—An underwater robot with a T.V. camera for eyes and sonar pingers for ears. It is operated by a man on a ship above. Mr. Mobot is pushed by propellers.

► Diving Cylinders
   1. Bathysphere
   2. Benthoscope
   3. Bathyscaphe
   4. Trieste I and II
   5. Mesocaph
   6. Denise
   7. Alvin
   8. Aluminaut

► Equipment

1. Aqualung—metal oxygen tank
2. Diving suit—helps men explore water around the 500 foot level
3. Submarine—underwater ship
4. Fathometer—used to trace ocean floor—sound waves sent to ocean floor—bounce back a signal to ship and the signal is recorded on a moving strip of paper.
5. Hydrophones—an underwater listening device to record sounds in the water
6. Nasen Bottle—used to obtain water samples
7. Bathythermograph—used to determine water temperature

Informational Activities

• Have students make a chart of the equipment and the supplies that aquanauts need and use. Attempt to get pictures of these from magazines and newspapers.
• Art work. Have youngsters design underwater diving gear and underwater ships and spheres. Have them explain the purpose of the modifications they make. Plan an exhibit of the designs.

Culminating the Unit—Summarizing Activities

■ Prepare a school display for all other classes to see.
■ Prepare a skit for other grades depicting the problems and results of Sealab II.
■ Have students continually follow up the unit by keeping a record of all other activities and new developments that they read about.
■ Prepare a class newspaper on oceanography for teachers, parents, and other students.
■ Have students prepare a "television documentary" using an eight mm. camera. Have them take pictures of the room displays, skits, experiments, projects, etc. Show the film at a P.T.A. meeting or invite parents to the classroom to view the film.

■ Visit an aquarium or other place where fish are displayed.
■ Start an aquarium in the classroom, discussing the essential features for maintaining living things in the water.

Evaluation Techniques

Observation of Youngsters

1. During discussion—
   (*a*) Interest   (*b*) Contributions

2. During experiments—
   (*a*) Use of materials   (*b*) Participation
                (*c*) Making inferences

3. During group work—
   (*a*) Works effectively with others
   (*b*) Makes a contribution to the group's efforts

4. During individual projects—
   (*a*) Interest   (*b*) Initiative

Written Test on Information Gained in the Unit

DIRECTIONS: Underline the correct answer.

1. The earth is to geology what the sea is to
   (*a*) *oceanography*   (*c*) aquanauts
   (*b*) fish   (*d*) biology

2. The moon is to tides what the wind is to
   (*a*) the equator   (*c*) *currents*
   (*b*) heat   (*d*) sun

3. A member of the aquanaut team of Sealab II who is also an astronaut is
   (*a*) Jacques Piccard   (*c*) Bob Sonnenberg
   (*b*) *Scott Carpenter*   (*d*) George Bond

4. A parallel is to latitude what a _____ is to longitude.
   (*a*) maritime   (*c*) equator
   (*b*) pole   (*d*) *meridian*

5. A thermometer is to the air, and an electrocardiogram is to the heart, what a _____ is to the water.
   (*a*) hydrophone   (*c*) *bathythermograph*
   (*b*) guyot   (*d*) bathysphere

DIRECTIONS: Complete the following sentences.

1. The ruggedness of the ocean floor might be compared to
   _____.

2. It has been said that oceanography is a new science that attempts to _____.

3. Exploring outer space is similar to exploring the depths of the sea because _____.

4. The symbiotic and parasitic relationship among marine life can be explained by _____
   _____.

5. The following conditions affect life in the sea: _____
   _____.

DIRECTIONS: In one or more paragraphs, discuss the following:

1. Using your own words, describe what seem to be the major problems of ocean study.

2. Why might the oceans be considered a "pot of gold" in man's quest for resources?

3. Oceanography is a *new* science, but men have been exploring the depths of the ocean since 1934. Outline some of the major investigations and relate their main purpose.

4. Is it more important for man to study "inner space" or "outer space"? Support your position.

5. Explain why ocean water is salty and inland water is fresh.

OCEANOGRAPHY

References for Children

1. Adler, Irving and Ruth. *Oceans.* New York: John Day Co., 1962.
2. Arnov, Boris. *Wonders of the Deep Sea.* New York: Dodd, Mead & Co., 1959.
3. Buehr, Walter. *World Beneath the Waves.* New York: W. W. Norton and Co. Inc., 1964.
4. Burton, Maurice. *Life Under the Sea.* London: Spring Books, 1961.

5. Clarke, Arthur. *Challenge of the Sea.* New York: Holt, Rinehart and Winston, 1960.
6. Colby, C. B. *Submarine.* New York: Coward-McCann, Inc., 1960.
7. Coombs, Charles. *Deep-Sea World: The Story of Oceanography.* New York: William Morrow and Company, 1966.
8. Del Rey, Lester. *The Mysterious Sea.* Philadelphia: Chilton Co., 1961.
9. Ellis, Anabel. *The Unknown Ocean.* New York: G. P. Putnam's Sons, 1959.
10. Epstein, Samuel. *The Real Book About the Sea.* New York: Garden City Books, 1954.
11. Epstein, Sam and Beryl. *The First Book of the Ocean.* New York: Franklin Watts, Inc., 1961.
12. Engel, Leonard. *The Sea.* Life Nature Library. New York: Time-Life, Inc., 1962.
13. Fisher, James. *Wonderful World of the Sea.* New York: Garden City Books, 1957.
14. Knowlton, W. *Let's Explore Beneath the Sea.* New York: Knopf Publishing Co., 1957.
15. Lane, F. C. *All About the Sea.* New York: Random House, 1963.
16. Ray, Carleton. *Wonders of the Living Sea.* New York: Home Library Press, 1963.
17. Meyer, Jerome. *Picture Book of the Sea.* New York: Lothrop, Lee, and Shepard Co. Inc., 1956.
18. Schraff, Robert. *How and Why Wonder Book of Oceanography.* New York: Grosset and Dunlap, 1964.
19. Selsam, Millicent and Morrow, Betty. *See Through the Sea.* New York: Harper and Brothers, 1955.
20. Sherman, Diane. *You and the Oceans.* Chicago: Childrens Press, 1965.

References for Teachers

1. Bascom, W. *A Hole in the Bottom of the Sea.* Garden City, New York: Doubleday, 1961.
2. Carrington, Richard. *A Biography of the Sea.* New York: Basic Books, Inc., 1960.
3. Carson, Rachel. *The Sea Around Us.* New York: Oxford University Press, 1961.

4. Clarke, Arthur. *The Challenge of the Sea.* New York: Henry Holt Co., 1960.
5. Colman, John. *The Sea and Its Mysteries.* New York: Norton and Co., Inc., 1950.
6. Cowen, Robert. *Frontiers of the Sea: The Story of Oceanographic Expeditions.* New York: Doubleday and Co., Inc., 1960.
7. Cramie, W. J. *Exploring the Secrets of the Sea.* Englewood Cliffs, New Jersey: Prentice-Hall, Inc., 1962.
8. Deacon, George. *Seas, Maps, and Men: An Atlas History of Man's Expeditions of the Oceans.* New York: Doubleday and Co., Inc., 1962.
9. Douglas, John. *The Story of the Ocean.* New York: Dodd, Mead and Co., 1952.
10. Engel, Leonard. *The Sea.* New York: Time-Life, Inc., 1967.
11. Guberlet, Muriel. *Explorers of the Sea.* New York: Ronald Press Co., 1964.
12. Hull, Seabrook. *The Bountiful Sea.* Englewood Cliffs, New Jersey: Prentice-Hall, Inc., 1964.
13. Yasso, Warren E. *Oceanography.* New York: Holt, Rinehart and Winston, Inc., 1965.

Charts

Study the Ocean Depths. New York: Scott, Foresman and Co. "Oceanology" *Instructor.* Free. May 1965, p. 69.

Periodicals

1. Cousteau, Jacques-Yves. "Working for Weeks on the Sea Floor." *National Geographic.* 129:498-537. April 1966.
2. Johnson, W. "Man's Future Beneath the Sea." *Senior Scholastic.* 85:6-8. January 7, 1965.
3. Link, E. A. "Tomorrow on the Deep Frontier." *National Geographic.* 125:778-801. June 1964.
4. "Man in the Sea." *Teaching Trends.* New York: Scott, Foresman and Company. Free. 1966.
5. "Out of the Sea." *World Book Year Book Reprint.* Chicago: Field Enterprise Educational Corp., 1963.
6. "Scraping the Bottom; New Deposits of Metals on the Ocean Floor." *Newsweek.* 61:66. April 15, 1963.

7. Stark, Walter A. "Marvels of a Coral Realm." *National Geographic*. 130:710-738. November 1966.
8. "The Living Ocean." *World Book Year Book Reprint*. Chicago: Field Enterprises Educational Corp., 1963.
9. Wolfert, I. "Ocean Currents: How the World's Bloodstream Flows." *Popular Science*. 183:76-8. August 1963.

Index

A

Abbreviations, 23, 28
Acceleration and deceleration, 164, 189
Action-reaction principle, 166-168, 176-177
Advertisments, 25-26, 125
  key words, 26
Air pollution, 87, 91-94
  causes of, 91-92
  developing unit, 91-94
  informational activities, 91-94
  objectives, 91
  smog, 92-93
Air pressure, effects of, 180
Alphabetical order, 57
  dictionaries, 59
Animals, 10, 98-99
  in danger of extinction, 91
  wildlife preservation, 110-116
    (see also Wildlife Preservation)
Apollo program, 156, 168, 175-184
  action-reaction, 166-168, 176-177
  evaluation techniques, 182-184
  informational activities, 176-187
  moon landing, 176, 178-179
  motivational activities, 176
  objectives of unit, 175
  tests and testing, 182-184
Aquanauts, 157, 212, 214
Aquariums, 215

Arithmetic:
  catalogues used, 48-52
  graphs and charts, 15, 85
  intermediate grades:
    use of catalogues, 48-52
    use of road maps, 30, 36-40
    use of travel folders, 81-85
  primary grades, 81
    use of road maps, 30, 35-36
  problems, 11-16, 38-40, 81-86, 149
  Roman numerals, 14
  use of advertisements, 11-13
  use of catalogues, 47-52
  use of newspapers, 10-16
  use of road maps, 30, 35-40
    estimating distances, 36
    for mathematical concepts, 21, 35-36
  use of telephone directories, 58
  use of travel folders, 81-85
Art projects, 26, 113
  scale drawings, 27-28
  space exploration, 163, 191
Assembly programs, on water pollution, 101
Assignments, use of travel folders, 71
Astronauts, 156-157, 184-200
  evaluation techniques, 194-196
  food problems, 191-192
  motivational activities, 185
  objectives of unit, 185
  qualifications, 187-188

Astronauts (con't.)
  reference material, 196-197
  selection of, 186-187
  space suits, 190-191
  survival in space, 190-193
  tests and testing, 194-196
  training, 185, 186, 188-190
Astronomy, 190
Atlases, 69
Atmosphere, 159
Auctions, 125-126
Automobiles, buying, 141

B

Balance of nature, 110-111, 112
Banks and banking, 119, 127-135
  checking accounts, 131-132
  credit unions, 127
  definition, 129
  evaluation techniques, 134
  Federal Reserve System, 127,
    132-133
  informational activities, 128-133
  kinds of banks, 128-129
  loans, 130-132
  mortgages, 131
  motivational activities, 128
  occupations, 127, 134
  reference material, 135-136
  savings accounts, 128, 130-131
Barter system, 120
Biographies, in encyclopedias, 67
Book reviews, 22
Boston Tea Party, 148, 153
Brainstorming, 104, 191
Bulletin board displays, 8, 9, 26,
    34, 63
  astronauts, 185, 188
  banks, 132
  credit plans, 138
  oceanography, 201, 209
  on science, 8
  on soil conservation, 108
  space exploration, 167
  taxes, 50

C

Careers, 108
  in banking, 127, 134
  in space exploration, 187, 194

Cartoons, 3-4, 24-25, 109
Catalogues, 46, 47-54
  for arithmetic problems, 48-52
  developing skill in using, 47-54
  ordering merchandise, 48
  for vocabulary building, 53
Centrifugal force, 156, 164-165
Checking accounts, 131-132
Comparisons, teaching, 36-37
Conservation units, 87-118
  air pollution, 87, 91-94
  background information, 88
  balance of nature, 110-111, 112
  debates, 90, 94
  exhibits, 90
  initiating activities, 88
  national parks, 88
  natural resources, 87
  objectives of unit, 88-89
  posters on, 90, 94
  reference material on, 116-118
  soil conservation, 87, 104-110
  sources of information on, 89-
    90
  stimulating interest in, 88
  vocabulary building and, 90-91
  water pollution, 87, 94-104
  wildlife preservation, 88, 110-
    116
Credit, 119, 135-145
  advantages and disadvantages,
    139-140
  bank loans versus, 141
  bankruptcy, 143
  book credit, 138, 139
  budgets, 142
  contract plan, 138
  credit cards, 135, 138-139, 141
  credit ratings, 136, 137, 138
  evaluation techniques, 144-145
  informational activities, 137-143
  installment buying, 136, 138-
    139
  interest charges, 136, 140, 141
  motivational activities, 136
  objectives of unit, 136-137
  reference material, 145
  reports on, 144
  thrift, 136, 140, 142
Credit unions, 127
Currents, ocean, 206-207

D

Debates, 187
  on air pollution, 90, 94
  on conservation, 90, 94
  on credit, 144
  newspaper articles for, 5
  on oceanography, 212
Dictionary study, 46, 59-62
  alphabetical order, 57, 59
  arrangement, 59
  games, 59-60
  guide words, 62
  root words, 59
  using road maps, 41-42
Dioramas, 9, 115, 210
Directions, 32, 33
  following, 28
Discussion techniques, 41
Distances, estimating, 36
Dramatizations, 6, 7, 40
  on banking, 132
  on credit, 141, 143-144
  newspaper articles, 6
  on oceanography, 212, 214
  puppet shows, 141, 148, 151
  space exploration, 168, 182
  supply and demand, 122, 125
  on taxes, 148
  travelogue for television pro-
    grams, 80
  travel skits, 80

E

Ecology of animals and plants, 98-
  99
Economics, 119-155
  banks and banking, 119, 127-135
  change and growth, 119
  consumption, 124-125
  credit, 119, 135-145
  free enterprise system, 119, 123
  gross national product (GNP),
    119, 124
  reference material, 127, 145,
    154-155
  relationship to government, 119
  supply and demand, 119, 120-
    127
  taxes, 119, 146-155

Encyclopedias, 46, 63-69
  arrangement, 63
  biographies in, 66-67
  developing skill in using, 63-69
  locating material in, 63-64
  parts of speech, 67
  punctuation, 67
Exhibits, 90, 153
Experience charts, 40

F

Fact sheets, 92-93, 153
Farming methods, 105-107
  effect on soil conservation, 105-
    106
Federal Reserve System, 127, 132-
  133
Field trips, 75
  to aquariums, 215
  outdoor study, 89
  to telephone office, 58
  use of maps for, 32
Films:
  on economics, 122, 128-130,
    133, 153
  on newspapers, 18
  on oceanography, 201, 208, 210-
    213
  on soil conservation, 105, 107,
    108
  on space exploration, 158, 159,
    160, 162, 176, 179, 180,
    182, 186, 189-193
  on water pollution, 97, 102
  on wildlife preservation, 111,
    113, 114, 115
Fishing industry, 95, 96, 98-99,
  209
Floor plans, 27-28
Food and meals, 28-29, 191-192
Free enterprise system, 119, 123

G

Games:
  dictionary study, 59-60
  use of road maps, 33-34, 42-44
Gemini project, 175, 176
Graphs and charts, 85, 150
  bar and pie graphs, 85
  construction of, 15, 123

Graphs and charts (con't.)
  supply and demand, 123
  weather, 74
Gravity, 156, 160-163, 176, 178-179
  G-forces, 179-180
Gross national product (GNP), 119, 124

H

Health habits, 95, 188

I

Illustrations, news stories, 4
Industrial revolution, 94, 99
Inertia, 156, 164, 178
Insecticides and pesticides, 99
Installment buying, 136, 138-139
Interest, bank, 119, 130, 136, 140, 141
Intermediate grades:
  arithmetic
    use of road maps, 36-40
  language arts:
    use of newspapers, 3-6
    use of road maps, 41-44
  magazines, 20-29
  reference books, 47
  social studies, 72
    use of road maps, 32-34
Interstate highways, 34
Interviews and interviewing, 6, 186, 187
  questions for, 137
  on taxes, 146, 148
Irrigation, 95

L

Landscape information, 28
Language arts:
  creative writing, 41, 78, 163
  developing skills, 76-77
  dramatizations (*see* **Dramatizations**)
  figurative language, 3-4, 20, 76-77
  getting main idea, 20-21
  intermediate grades:
    use of road maps, 41-44

Language arts (con't.)
  travel folders, 75-80
  use of magazines, 20-29
  use of newspapers, 3-6
  letter-writing, 75, 80
  primary grades:
    use of newspapers, 2-3
    use of road maps, 40-41
  punctuation, 67
  sentence structure, 79-80
  space exploration, 185, 188, 194
  use of catalogues, 53-54
  use of dictionaries, 59-62
  use of encyclopedias, 63-69
  use of magazines, 20-29
  use of newspapers, 3-6
  use of road maps, 40-44
  use of telephone directories, 56-58
  use of travel folders, 75-80
  use of Yellow Pages, 54-57
  word study, 75-80
Latitude and longitude, 202-204
Lawson, Robert, 111
Letter-writing:
  on air pollution, 95
  letters to the editor, 6
  road map study and, 40, 42
  use of catalogues, 54
  use of travel folders, 75, 80
  use of Yellow Pages, 56
Loans, 119, 130-132, 141

M

Magazines, 19-29, 185
  advertisements, 25-26
  analysis of, 22
  book reviews, 22
  cartoons, 24-25
  compared with newspapers, 24
  editorials, 23-24
  for educational and recreational reading, 20
  figurative and picturesque language, 20
  materials and resources, 20
  objectives, 19
  picture reading, 26
  reference material, 29
  structure and organizations of, 20, 22

Magazines (con't.)
  use in intermediate grades, 20-29
  use in primary grades, 20
  using effectively, 19
  weekly news, 24
Mail:
  parcel post zones, 49
  zip code area maps, 57
Maps and map-making:
  legends on, 31-32
  primary grades, 31-32
  use of atlases, 69
  use of travel folders, 72
Mental health, 188
Merchandise catalogues, 46, 47-54
    (*see also* Catalogues)
Mercury project, 175, 176
Meridians, 203-204
Mileage, computing, 37-38
Minerals, in ocean, 209
Models, construction, 182
Money, 120
Moon landing, 156, 176, 178-179
Mortgages, 131, 136, 139
Mythology, Greek and Roman, 68

N

Natural resources, 87 (*see also* Conservation)
  conservation of, 87-88
  in ocean, 209-210
Newspaper study, 1-18, 109
  advertisements, 3, 7
  arithmetic, 10-16
  business and financial section, 7-8
  cartoons, 3
  class or school, 2, 16, 93, 214
  entertainment features, 3
  factual news reporting, 3
  file of special articles, 8
  format and style, 6
  headlines, 3, 5
  human interest stories, 3
  illustrations, 4
  in intermediate grades, 3
  language arts, 3-6
  objectives of unit, 1-2
  in primary grades, 2-3
  references, 16-18
  science, 8-10
  social studies, 6-8

Newspaper study (con't.)
  to stimulate interest, 1-18
  syndicated columns, 3
Newton, Sir Isaac, 163, 166-167, 177
  First Law of Motion, 177
  Third Law of Motion, 166-167
Note-taking, 5
Notebooks:
  on oceanography, 201, 210
  on science, 9
  on space program, 162
  travel, 72, 74, 85
  word lists, 5
Numbers, reading and writing, 81

O

Oceanography, 157, 200-219
  aquanauts, 212, 214
  characteristics of ocean, 201-202, 204-206
  devices and equipment, 211, 213-214
  effect of water pressure, 212-213
  evaluation techniques, 215-216
  explorations, 211-214
  informational activities, 201-204
  latitude and longitude, 202-204
  meridians, 203-204
  motivational activities, 201
  nature of, 201-202
  notebooks on, 201, 210
  objectives of unit, 200
  ocean currents, 206-207
  reference material, 216-219
  research, 211-212
  resources, 209-210
  tests and testing, 215-216
  tides, 208
  waves, 207-208
Orbits, 156, 160, 165-166, 178-179
  perigee and apogee, 166
Outlines, 5-6, 21
Oxygen, necessary for burning, 161

P

Panel discussions, 115, 187
  on conservation, 90
Perigee and apogee, 166

Picture collections, 26
    use of travel folders for, 73
Planets, 159
Plants:
    ecology of animals and, 98-99
    transpiration, 97, 98
Posters:
    on conservation, 90, 94
    constructing, 56
    contests, 143
    on proper use of telephone, 58
    soil conservation, 106, 108
    on thrift, 143
    travel, 76
    water pollution, 96, 97, 99, 103
Prefixes and suffixes, 5, 59-60
Preservation, 88 (see also Wildlife
    preservation)
Prices and pricing, 123-124
    consumption and, 125
    equilibrium price, 123-124
Primary grades:
    arithmetic, 35-36
    language arts, 40-41
        use of newspapers, 2-3
        use of road maps, 40-41
    magazines, 20
    newspaper study, 2-3
    reference books, 47
    travel folders, 72
Project Apollo (see Apollo pro-
    gram)
Public speaking, 40

R

Radiation, 100
Radio programs, 109, 144
Rainmakers, 97
Reading:
    for content, 2, 3
    for discrimination, 2
    educational and recreational, 20
    magazines, 20
    newspapers, 2, 3
    travel folders, 75
Recreation, 95, 96
Reference books, 46-70
    atlases, 46, 69
    dictionaries, 46, 59-62
    encyclopedias, 46, 63-69
    intermediate grades, 47

Reference books (con't.)
    merchandise catalogues, 46, 47-
        54
    objectives, 47
    primary grades, 47
    reference material on, 70
    skills needed to use, 46-70
    telephone directories, 46, 56-58
    Yellow Pages, 46, 54-56
Resource persons, 108, 151
Rivers, study of, 104
Road maps, study of, 30-45
    arithmetic, 30, 35-40
    games:
        "Across the Border," 34
        "anagrams," 42
        "Find It," 33-34
        scrambled words, 43
        "Where is it?" 44
    intermediate grade activities, 31,
        32-34
    interstate highways, 34
    language arts, 30, 40-44
    legends on, 31-32, 33
    locating places on, 33
    objectives, 30
    primary grade activities, 31-32
    social studies, 30, 31-35
Rockets, 156, 160-162, 164, 166-
    168
    acceleration, 164
    action-reaction principle, 166-
        168
    propellants, 166
    Saturn V, 166, 168
    step principle, 161-162

S

Satellites, 156, 160, 164-166
    communication, 182
Saturn V rocket engine, 166, 168
Science:
    outside speakers, 9
    use of magazines, 22-23
    use of newspapers, 8-10
Scientific method, 177
Sealab II, 157, 214
Seashells, 210
Sentence structure, 79-80
    diagraming, 79-80
    magazines, 20-21

Sentence structure (con't.)
  painting, 79
  topic sentences, 5, 20-21
Sewage, 94
  water pollution and, 99, 103-104
Smog, 92-93
Social studies:
  atlas, 69
  encyclopedias, 64-65
  intermediate grades, 72-75
    use of newspapers, 6-8
    use of road maps, 32-34
    use of travel folders, 72-75
  primary grades, 72
    use of road maps, 31-32
  travel folders, use of, 72-75
    benefits of traveling, 74
    collections of, 72, 75
    compared with road maps, 73
    cultural activities, 74
    famous people and, 74
    famous vacation spots, 73
    field trips, 75
    to illustrate outline maps, 72
    for picture collections, 73-74
    planning trips, 72
    transportation, types of, 75
  use of newspapers for, 6-8
Soil conservation, 87, 104-110
  careers in, 108
  Dust Bowl, 104, 106
  effect of farming methods, 105-
    107
  effect on water pollution, 99,
    100-101
  erosion control, 105
  evaluation techniques, 109-110
  ground cover, 102-103
  methods, 106
  newspaper on, 109
  objectives of unit, 104-105
  posters, 106, 108
  resource persons, 108
  U.S. Soil Conservation Service,
    107
Solar system, 193
Space exploration, 156-175
  acceleration and deceleration,
    164, 189
  aerospace science, 156
  Apollo program, 175-184 (see
    also Apollo program)

Space exploration (con't.)
  astronauts, 156-157, 184-200
    (see also Astronauts)
  atmosphere, 159
  basic concepts, 157-175
  careers in, 187, 194
  centrifugal force, 156, 164-165
  characteristics of space, 159
  evaluation techniques, 169-175
  file of special articles on, 8-9
  gravity, 156, 160-163, 176, 178-
    179
  inertia, 156, 164, 178
  jet engines, 161
  language arts activities, 185, 188
    194
  moon landing, 156, 176, 178-179
  motivational activities, 158
  NASA, 168
  notebooks, 162
  objectives of unit, 157
  orbits, 156, 160, 165-166
  payloads, 161, 165
  perigee and apogee, 166
  reference material, 196-200
  rockets, 156, 160-162, 164, 166-
    168
  satellites, 156, 160, 164-166
  speed to overcome gravity, 163-
    166
  stages, 168
  survival in space, 190-193
  tests and testing, 169-175
  thrust, 168
  vocabulary development, 158,
    160, 161, 189
Spelling, 5, 9
  credit game, 136
Summarizing, magazine articles, 21
Supply and demand, 119, 120-127
  equilibrium price, 123-124
  evaluation techniques, 126
  films, 122
  informational activities, 121-125
  meaning of, 121-123
  motivational activities, 120-121
  objectives, 120
  reference material, 127

T

Taxes, 119, 146-155
  arithmetic problems, 149

Taxes (con't.)
  collections, 150
  evaluation techniques, 153-154
  fact sheet, 153
  Federal budget, 150
  government supported by, 147-149
  income tax, 146, 151-153
  informational activities, 147-153
  kinds of, 148-149
  motivational activities, 146-147
  need for, 147-148
  objectives of unit, 146
  property tax, 151
  reference material, 154-155
  resource people, 151
  state and local, 150
  tax base, 146
  tests and testing, 153-154
  withholding tax, 146, 152
Teaching aids:
  newspapers, 1-18
  magazines, 19-29
  reference books, 46-70 (see also Reference books)
  road maps, 30-45
  travel folders, 71-86
Telephone directories, 46, 56-58
  alphabetical order, 57
  area code numbers, 56
  arrangement, 56
  developing skill in using, 56-58
  emergency calls, 56-57
  long distance rates, 58
  overseas calls, 58
  proper usage of telephone, 56-57, 58
  "Tele-Trainer" kits, 58
  zip code area map, 57
Television programs:
  on banks, 134
  documentaries, 214
  on oceanography, 214
  preparing travelogues for, 80
  space exploration, 181-182
Tests and testing:
  conservation unit, 109-110
  oceanography, 215-216
  space program, 169-175
  supply and demand, 126
  taxes, 153-154
  wildlife preservation, 116

Thrift, 136, 140, 142
Tides and waves, 207-208
Town meetings, 151
Trading posts, 121
Transpiration, 97-98
Transportation, 95
  airplanes, 74
  use of travel folders, 75
Travel folders, 71-86
  arithmetic instruction, 81-85
  assignments, 71
  benefits of travel, 74
  collections of, 72, 75
  creative writing, 78
  descriptive language, 71
  interesting pictures, 71
  in intermediate grades, 72
  for language arts, 75-80
  materials and resources, 72
  to motivate students, 71
  notebooks, 72, 74, 85
  objectives, 71
  in primary grades, 72
  reference material, 85-86
  social studies, 72-75
  types of transportation, 74

U

United States:
  Fish and Wildlife Service, 114
  Internal Revenue Service, 148
  Soil Conservation Service, 107

V

Van Allen radiation belt, 193
Verb study, use of travel folders, 80
Vocabulary building:
  conservation unit, 90-91
  space program, 158, 160, 161, 180, 189
  use of catalogues, 53
  use of newspapers, 5-6
  use of road maps, 40, 41

W

Water pollution, 87, 94-104
  causes, 95, 99-101
  detergents, 99-100

Water pollution (con't.)
  heat, 100
  industry, 94, 98, 99
  insecticides and pesticides, 99
  radiation, 100
  sewage, 99, 103-104
  silt, 99, 100
  conservation of water resources,
    101-104
  ground cover, 102-103
  purification methods, 101-102,
    104
  effects of industrial revolution,
    94, 99
  fishing industry, 95, 96, 98-99,
    209
  ground water, 96
  informational activities, 95-104
  objectives of unit, 95
  recreation and, 95, 96
  sources of water, 96
  surface water, 96, 200
  transpiration, 97, 98
  value of water, 95-96
  wastes and sewage, 94, 99
  water cycle, 95, 96, 97
  water drought, 95
  watershed, 97
  water table, 97
  waterways, 95
Water pressure, 212-213
Weather maps and forecasts, 9, 15,
    74, 182
Weight and mass, 163
Weightlessness, 179-180, 189, 191
Wildlife preservation, 110-116
  agencies and organizations, 111,
    113-115
  balance of nature, 110-111, 112
  bird watchers club, 112
  evaluation techniques, 116
  extinct animals, 110, 113
  game refuges, 115
  importance of, 112

Wildlife preservation (con't.)
  informational activities, 112-116
  initiating unit, 111-112
  legislation affecting, 113-114,
    115
  motivating students, 111-112
  objectives of unit, 111
  projects on, 115-116
Word study (see also Vocabulary
    building)
  compound words, 55
  derivations, 5, 202
  dictionaries, 59-62
  encyclopedias, 67
  magazines for, 21
  newspapers, 5
  prefixes and suffixes, 5
  root words, 5, 59
  science notebook, 9
  syllabication, 5
  synonyms, homonyms, and anto-
    nyms, 78-79
  use of newspapers, 5-6
  use of travel folders, 75-79
Writing, 2, 4
  on air pollution, 93, 95
  creative, 41, 163
    travel folders, 78
  letter-writing (see Letter-writ-
    ing)
  magazine articles, 21-22
  newspaper articles, 6
  poems and stories, 129

Y

Yellow Pages, 46, 54-56
  compound words, 55
  developing skills in using, 54-56
  locating material, 54-55

Z

Zip code area maps, 57